Over the Years I Found Peace
God's Presence Quiets My Mind

By Barbara Lee Laubert

A Mother's Yearning & Thankfulness
Along the Path of Life

Bilbo Books Publishing
www.BilboBooks.com
bilbobookspublishing@gmail.com
(706)-549-1597

ISBN 979-8-9867043-6-4

Printed in the United States of America
All rights reserved. Published in the United States of America by
Bilbo Books Publishing. Athens, Georgia

Cover Illustration & Frontispiece
My Lily (2008), 2' x 4' oil painting
by Barbara L. Laubert

)))))))))))**** Forward ****(((((((((((

The reason for writing this book has been to share my many poems and more. Thought provoking readings, with hopes I can inspire others to know the **Lord** and His work in my life and **yours**. **My trust and belief in God** has guided me through many trials and challenges. **God** blessed me with a wonderful, supportive husband who has encouraged me to put together this book. We have nine children, many of the poems are about them. I've been writing for 65 plus years so far.

Two and a half years ago I nearly passed away. It just wasn't my time to go, but I am still on hospice care. It is through the goodness of my splendid care that the hospice team offered me a UGA graduate to help compile my work. This has been the best medicine in hleping me recover thus far. It took my mind off of myself. Hospice covers every aspect of your health. This work has been a big part of getting better.

I am 90 years old and have been married for 71 years. Wow!

I am so blessed!

Plesse enjoy my work and journey over the years.

My best, Barbara L. Laubert

Table of Contents

Chapter 5
***During the Winter
    of My Life***

Chapter 6:
Laudable Entries

Epilogue

Dedication

This book is dedicated to my husband Andy. He is the love of my life, my support and the one who has encouraged me to publish my book of poems. It has been a collection over the past 65 years. Covering the 70 years of marriage and raising nine children to adulthood. Our family now numbers 71 members in all.

I admire the fabulous talent my man has, working with all kinds of wood. He can build houses and the entire useful finishing touches in a home, that any woman would dream of and more. Even 48"–7' shutters for an antebellum home or making wider treads for about 12 steps, so a tall woman's shoes could step comfortably and safely to the second story of her home. He has done work for so many people that I can not count them all.

Andy has transformed our double-wide trailer completely into a lovely rancher inside and out. He built magnificent dark wood kitchen cabinets with many extras for my convenience to work safely and easily. I am a blessed woman to have such an ambitious man. Our grandson Ronan calls his grand-pop "The Builder Man." And believe me Andy is.

We live in the country, on almost 2 acres of land. Up until now Andy has maintained the whole yard, built a wall in back of the house and a large arbor out front covered with bright yellow Carolina Jasmine. Our place is called "Paradise Found."

Today he is 91—he is finally watching TV and taking a rest. I consider Andy to be exceptional because of his extra ordinary ability, conscientious attention to whatever job his work entails. Including restoring antique furniture, such as carving, or lathe work. He can do it well!

Above all else, Andy has been the ideal husband. Loving, kind and caring for all of us.

Thank you my dear—I'll always love you.
Toots (Barbara L. Laubert)

>>>> **Who Could Love Me More?** <<<<
{Andy}

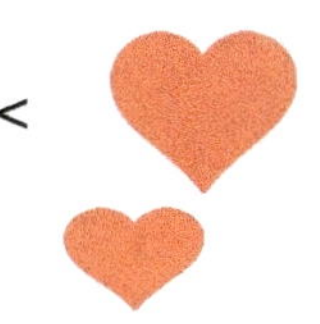

I have a man, who's just right for me,
He has hugs and kisses and fills me with glee.
I need to express, all the love that's inside,
So happy I took him for that very first ride.

I appreciate how well he's taken care of me,
Plus our nine kids, it's been quite a journey.
He's always provided a safe car,
So I could travel, no matter how far.

Over the years he continues to build,
His work should be in the builders' guild.
One home after another with pride I exclaim,
A job well done and mention his name.

Often he'll bring me a sweet little gift,
Showing his love always gives me a lift.
My man, he's still working at eighty-six,
People are asking about things to be fixed.

Oh how I love this guy, who has many abilities,
He works them effortlessly and with such ease.
From the day we met, 'till I was his bride,
For 72 years now, by each other's side.

Acknowledgments

First of all I want to thank my children: Andy, Ruthie, Gracie, Rosemary, Billy, Lori, Doug, Bevie and Greg. It is through my LOVE for each one, that I wrote these poems. My desire to have a large family was granted by the LORD and my dear Andy, my hubby. Thank you dear family for working on meeting the needs of we old folks.

Many, many people over the years who volunteered their time and care to give us hand-me-down clothes, etc. has always been a huge help. My girlfriends who continue (even today), to have an ear over the past 69 years to share the happy times and those other times that I needed support.

These poems tell the story about my life and raising our large family. In April of 2020 I had fallen 6 times in the 6 weeks before hand. I wound up with Cellulitis in my right knee, I had broken a couple vertebrae—needed an operation and I was put on Hospice. This is 2022 and I 'm still using a hospital bed to relieve pain and swelling in my legs. Every one of my care-takers have proven to have their hearts in the right place. Not forgetting Ken Reed, our Chaplain with Inspiring Hospice, who is excellent. Thank you so much to all those who work for Inspiring Hospice.

In fact, it is through the *Inspiring Hospice Group;* namely in the office, for putting my latest poem, "When I pass to Eternal Life," on Facebook—receiving over 3,000 reviews. That has inspired me to put my poems into a book to get them published! Katie Courson has been my partner to see this work come to fruition. She has been a volunteer, working for Hospice. Katie is a college graduate and now working to become a geriatric social worker!

Many thanks to the friends from church, our wonderful neighbors and many dear friends for the visits, phone calls, food, gifts and Holy Communion. I must thank our good Lord for bringing me from near death to living again. Without HIS help I wouldn't have made it this far.

I hope I haven't forgotten anyone. If so, more thanks go out to you.

Most Sincerely,
Barbara L. Laubert

Front row: Beverly and Gregory.
Middle row: Rosemary, Billy, Barbara (Mom & Dad) Andy, plus
(Nana), Andy's Mother.
Back row: Douglas, Lori, Andy Jr., Grace, Ruthann.
This picture was taken in 1992—married 40 yrs.

Box 57, Galloway, NJ

Andy built the top 2 homes and completely rebuilt the house to the right.

430 Heidelberg Ave., Egg Harbor, NJ

Introduction

It was May first of 2021—I couldn't sleep,
A childhood prayer kept going through my head.
"Now I lay me down to sleep,"
kept repeating until I
got out of bed.

When I Pass to Eternal Life!

(Now I lay me down to sleep, to dream the dreams that I will reap.
With peace of mind, through the good Lord above, etc.
An Inspiring Hospice member took a copy of my
poem back to the office.
(See whole poem in chapter 5)

Many Thanks TOO

(Written about a poem I wrote called "When I Pass to Eternal Life")

Crystal Muench who read it and decided to put it on Facebook.
Over three thousand replies had the boss take a look.
The poem hit home in a magnificent way,
My volunteer Katie Courson comes on Friday.
We work together oh so well,
She finds the typos I goof, when I mis-spell.

This work occupies much of my time,
Finding the words that musically rhyme.

This inspiration has given me a BIG lift,
Sixty years later, oh what a gift!
To Publish my poems is an effort come true,
I send many thanks to **YOU and YOU!**

Chapter 1

Days of Youth & Innocence
Before The Grass Turns Green;
just getting started in the Adult World,
and so much to learn.

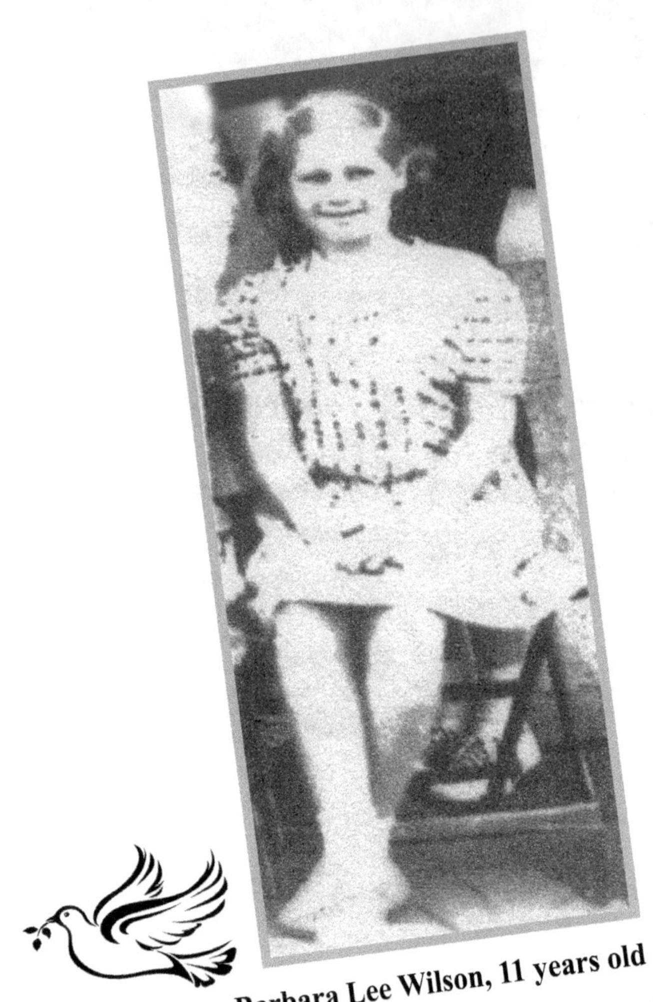

Barbara Lee Wilson, 11 years old

This is a 6th grade graduation picture. I had to go to the Academy of Holy names to boarding school in Tampa Florida the last half of sixth grade.

After having my tonsils out I continued ailing from a serious lung condition. Doctors advice was to send me somewhere with a warm climate.

After one year I was well and could go home to Philadelphia. (This was the last half of 1944 and first half of 1945.)

Did you ever try to remember as much as you could, about your own life experiences? It's fun!

And it feels mostly good inside. For me-my heart wells up and I want to cry. Yes that's me. I'm emotional, sensitive and I want everything to turn out right, for the good. It doesn't always work out that way.

This started out to be just my memories but, Father's Day is coming and I've been inspired to send these notes to my dad. He's 75 years old and maybe this will bring him a joy that's hard to express. One he'll remember and be happy to receive. 1512 Robinson Avenue: I think I was born here.

Easter baskets in the living room on the fireplace hearth. What fun to have so much candy. Um mm good! Then the time I hurt my chin when, I fell off the back porch into Mama's rock garden. My chin looked pretty bad so, I stood in back of the driver's seat holding cotton on my chin, while Daddy drove us to Delaware County Hospital. The doctor needed to put 3 stitches in to close the cut.

I remember an awful fight, Daddy and Mama had one day in Winter, when my Mama left home. She walked down the far away road, way in back of our house—across the big field. She had on her black fur coat. Daddy consoled us; by telling us she would come back. And Mama did come back home and we kids were mighty happy!

Daddy worked from home, his shop was downstairs in the basement of our home. Jack Ferguson worked for dad. I can still see the shop— how it was all set up and the smell I can imagine too. He rebuilt armatures that make motors run; like mixers and vacuum cleaners.

We knew Betty Ferguson; Jack's wife with her little one and Mama with we three kids, all went on a picnic to Darby Creek. Such fun! Boy, was that water cold as it rushed over small stones. This was a great day for all of us! Mama spread an old blanket on the ground where we had a tasty lunch. Peanut butter and jelly was a typical sandwhich back in 1938. And Mama made cupcakes for our treat.

At the bottom of the basement steps was an old wicker baby coach. I suppose it was for my sister Mary. She was two years younger than me. She and I were very different, I was a blonde; Mary was a brunette. I had blue eyes and she had green eyes. And our personalities were so opposite.

In 1939 I walked to Manoa School for 1st grade with Buddy who was in 5th grade. I can still see Buddy in his big furry robe as one of the three kings for the Christmas play. I sang Christmas songs with a group of other children. Then, the wonderful May Day celebration there too. What fun with many kids around the May Pole! Weaving long ribbons, each a different color, from the top of the pole, into a large circle. Everyone was hopping in and out that created a really nice design. I was only six years old, but I'll never forget that fun day.

Poor Barbara Repshaw—the time I hid her hat; I was sent to my room for teasing Barbara, but I did give her hat back! The big yellow bunny I picked all the fuzz off, while I was sucking my thumb. My parents thought I would never stop. And the time Mama broke the hair brush on the attic steps, going after Buddy who was running up the steps to his room, for teasing me.

One evening Mama and Daddy were visiting friends down the street. We could smell a motor burning and then the smoke. Buddy called the neighbor and Mama and Daddy came home. The situation was under control soon after Daddy took a look at the motor. Daddy knew just what to do about the burned up refrigerator motor.

In 1940 we moved to Llanerch, PA. I was 7 years old, a second grader. Oh—what a beautiful home! A giant living room with a fireplace. The breakfast nook that Daddy made the pretty three legged stools to go with the big breakfast bar. Each stool was a different color.

World War II was on so Mama's victory garden was across the street on a vacant lot and it yielded really good corn on the cob. I learned that

home grown broccoli can have little green worms in it. We washed out
the worms and we enjoyed the green veggie.

Another time a great impression was the tremendous effort to
remove all the old wall paper from the huge living room walls and up
the stairway to the second floor. When all the paper was soaked and
scrapped and the walls were ready—Dad painted. Oh how gorgeous!
It took quite a while to do that awful big job! Then finishing off the
attic with acoustical tile boards. My new, neat bedroom! A funny and
secretive happening up in that bedroom. I tried to smoke a cigarette—
Oh, how awful—I'm so glad I've never smoked since then.

On my 10th birthday my mama and daddy took me to Radio City
Music Hall in New York City, NY. The Rockette's with their red shoes.
A fabulous show!! Then on our return train ride home we had dinner
in the dining car. I said, "I wettened down my potatoes." Everybody
laughed so hard. Of course I was corrected. Daddy was a stickler for
proper language. We were never to ever say "GOT" or "TOOKEN."
Believe me we learned how to speak very fast!

In 1944 I took tap dance lessons and the gold metal dance recital
outfit. It was so scratchy! There was another outfit of crepe paper; I was
a flower in the dance recital. It turned out pretty good.

Then I took piano lessons—Mary took lessons too and we both
were in a recital. I never really learned how to play very well. But my
daughter Beverly plays beautifully today. I guess she had the inward
yearning to play like I felt, only Beverly made it happen..

I'll never forget the day Mama told me about our new baby on
the way.. She was sitting on the couch. The one with the stool under
one end of it, because it had a broken leg. This news was one of my
happiest moments.

This was 1944 when our new baby was born on April 22. The day
that Mama and Daddy brought Billy home was such a thrill. He was so
tiny and tan—he was peeling—because he was dehydrated. The cord
was in a knot before birth so he wasn't getting any nourishment shortly

before he was born. Now I felt like a little mother, only eleven years old.

Ugh! Dr. Diller—the killer—our dentist! Daddy would only take us to a dentist when we needed a tooth pulled. Oh, the pain! One time I had a big gum boil next to one of my teeth. It burst in my mouth. It was horrible!

Eleanor Menner and her mother and father (Menna and Gus.) My mama would often go there to enjoy "Motcha Cake (Motcha Kucken)" with Menna. I envied Ellie because she had to dry the dishes for only three people. I had to do dishes with my sister Mary (we were 6 all together for dinner) and it took much longer for us to finish our chore. When we were done we went back out to play. Ellie had red hair and there are so many more memories about the Menners. We have remained friends for over 81 years.

Mrs. Lewis with Lynn, her little girl. I wanted my own baby, but for some reason I had to wait until I grew up. Such loving memories about this family, for being allowed to baby sit for them at only eleven years old.

I remember walking across the big pipe to cross the creek at Conliff's back yard, to get to the rail-road tracks, which we walked on the way to school. Llanerch School - 2nd through 6th grade. This is where I broke my left arm. After school I was doing tricks on the see-saw. I stood up on the seat—lost my balance—fell and broke my arm. Again at school during recess, only 10 weeks later I was jumping rope, I fell again and broke the same arm in a different place. Delaware County Hospital again fixed me up.

One day I was talking to Barbara Betencourt from our side porch on Naylor's Run Road. I was angry about whatever she said and went to go back into the house, much too fast and put my hand through the window in the door. My neighbor Mrs, Yourtey, who lived next door to us knew First Aid. She put me together with adhesive tape butterflies and gauze. When Daddy came home he took me to Delaware County Hospital to have it redone, but the doctor said "leave it alone." "Mrs

Yourtey did a fine job." This was a cut about 6" long from the palm down over the wrist. Today I hardly have a scar.

We went to Ocean City most Sundays during the summers. When I was real little I would sleep on the shelf of the car. Or on a floor well in the back of the seat up front. But hardly ever on the back seat because my brother Buddy would get that place—after all he was the oldest! Four years older than me. Sometimes though, I did sit up front with Mama and Daddy.

I'll never forget the time I was punished and sent to my room. Mama was about to have baby Billy and Nana Harold was visiting— recuperating from a fall. She fell on a concrete flower pot and cut her face very bad. Well, she and Mama went into the attic to find baby clothes. Nana stepped off the floor boards and came through the ceiling into my bedroom. Her leg was dangling beside the light fixture. After getting Nana back on sound flooring once more, the three of us played Monopoly. I was forgiven—-Nana embarrassed—and Mama was a total wreck!

In September of 1944, I had my tonsils out—Wow! A throat I'll never forget! Mary and I were in the hospital at the same time I didn't get well. Back in the hospital again in November. A total of 56 penicillin shots in 9 days and 2 more days sitting on a rubber doughnut before I could go home. Christmas time came and the doctors' orders were—I'd have to go to Florida or Arizona to hopefully get my health back in good shape. Soooo—we were putting labels on everything from wash-clothes to underwear. Daddy took me to Tampa, Florida, to the Academy of Holy Names only five days after Christmas. Noel went with me, my doll. I was 11 years old. We traveled on the Silver Meteor train.

Aunt Alice and Uncle Charlie were so good to me. These people were friends of Nana Harold. I went to visit them on weekends while I lived in Florida. At Easter when Mama and Daddy brought Billy to see me, Billy took his first steps at Aunt Alice's. Then there was the Crystal Dining room in a hotel for lunch with my daddy and my girl friend Polly. At school I was allowed to pick oranges and grapefruit in the orchards in back of the school. So many memories while living at the academy. After living there for a year, I truly wanted to marry a Catholic man. God granted my wish.

One day when Mary and I had the chicken pox, both of us in our beds and all of a sudden—the ceiling fell, half of the ceiling came down—thank goodness it fell where we were not! More work for Dad or a repair man.

Then there was a hurricane that flooded our back yard and trees went down. Then the basement was flooded from the sewer backing up. Oh, what a mess! I had to throw away my stinky cast from my broken arm, with all the names on it. I had saved it in the toy closet Daddy built under the basement steps. I can still see that neat little toy closet. We lost almost everything in there.

Our Uncle Eddie who was in the Army, came home from World War II. He played the piano, just like always. He was really fun playing tricks with us kids too. We all enjoyed Daddy's brother, Uncle Eddie. He waited many years to marry Aunt Pearl,because of the war. They were married only 10 years when he had a severe heart attack and passed away. How sad and surely will be missed.

At Christmas of 1945 I was coming home for the holidays. I packed like I wouldn't have to go back to the Academy any more. Only thing was—I had to leave Noel behind because I didn't have enough room in my luggage. I traveled alone and I felt so bad leaving Noel behind. I loved the train ride and I remember staying awake for hours during the night. As we got further north the walls of the train became very cold. I watched and felt Summer turn into Winter in just 26 hours. I was so home sick that I packed as much of my belongings as I could to bring home. Maybe I could talk Mama and Daddy into not sending me back to the Academy after Christmas. It WORKED! I didn't have to go back. The only bad part was, I left Noel at the school and have felt like I abandoned her ever since. My consolation being; other little girls would have Noel to enjoy.

A new school—Haverford High School—It was enormous and easy to get lost in. I was twelve now, in seventh grade and felt so grown up. We walked to school about a mile and a half. Winter and Spring passed—Daddy sold our house on Naylor's Run Road—We moved to Egg Harbor City, NJ in August of 1946. A big old house at 546 Cincinnati Avenue. We had to have the house rewired because in some places there were still the original gas fixtures for lights. A new oil burner and had the plumbing repaired. This house had 4 small rooms in the basement with very low ceilings. The rooms were connected with dirt walls where a shelf was dug out. At Christmas time, Daddy put up our train set with the tracks running from room to room on that shelf. A very unusual basement. Really neat!

We also had 4 bedrooms upstairs, living and dining rooms and a large kitchen and bathroom on the first floor. Also a separate tiny room for the kitchen sink.

I can still picture the puppies with Bonnie our beautiful Collie. Bonnie had over 50 puppies in her lifetime.

Daddy also bought an old funeral home located at 245 Liverpool Avenue, to use for his armature factory, Wilson Armature Co. I worked for Dad when I was 17. I hooked up the armatures (it had to be done perfectly or the motor would not run). I also wound other armatures. Some were small enough to make dolls talk. Working for Dad gave me enough money to make the payments on the brand new car, a 1951 Nash Rambler, powder blue, convertible that Dad put the down payment on for my graduation gift and he also paid for the insurance. Gerry Frohman, Joanie Burley and myself had plenty of good times going to Philadelphia to canteen dances, the beach, playing hooky with Mom's help and I even drove to New York once, to help another girlfriend move to Egg Harbor.

Dad employed my girlfriends. Plus we went down the street from the factory, to Dye's Bakery to get Big Elephant EARS and other sweets at break time. We worked hard and we played hard!!

Nancy's mom, Mrs. Weisbecker, would drive Nancy, my Mama and me to the skating rink in Mays Landing, on Thursday nights. Our mothers would stay and watch, then take us home afterwards. Skating was one of the greatest joys of my life at that time. Not any more, in 1980 I skated for the last time. I went skating with my grand-children, to a benefit for the school. I fell and broke my left arm—for the third time and I broke the T5 vertebrae up near my neck. I was laid up for seven months soooo no more skating!

I graduated from Egg Harbor High School in 1951. On August 14, 1951 I met my extra special man. Six months after we met I married Andy Laubert on February 16,1952. We had a beautiful wedding! Mama and Daddy moved to Key Biscayne, Florida in 1953. I have never been able to accept the separation of family. For 32 years now, I have been telling myself that we all have our lives to lead in our own way, but somehow there's always something missing. My heart gets so heavy and there's no way to put the pieces into place the way you dreamed all about.

Life IS a Daydream

Life is a daydream, that doesn't work out,
The way you dreamed, and thought all about.
The road is so bumpy, the sea is so rough,
And making a living, is really tough.
We wanted a family, a big one and so,
Amongst all the joys, were many woes.
But one thing I'm sure of, at this jounrey's end,
The good Lord was with me, Yes, He is my friend.

By Barbara L. Laubert, nee Wilson 1993

Who knew that I would move to Georgia: just like my parents when they moved to Florida. **I followed my man!** Georgia is where he wanted to be for his retiremnet years. All of our adults now, were 30 years old plus, before we moved. Besides we came to where two of our daughters lived, along with many grand-children and great-grandchildren AND great-great-grandchildren live. 20 grand babies and 2 of our own children have settled here in the south. Life IS a Daydream!

YOU NEVER REALLY KNOW THE PATHS THAT LIFE WILL TAKE YOU!!!!

When we met August 14, 1951 [Andy Laubert & Barbara Wilson]

The little Blue Convertible Rambler, 1951.
Andy came up to my window and said,
**   "When are you going to take me for a ride?"**

~~~~ **When We Met** ~~~~

I love you oh so very much, more than words can say,
I'm glad I took you for a ride when you came up to me that day.
And furthermore when you stood me up, which was our
very first date,

I found you and we did go out to the boardwalk,
though it was quite late.

You won my heart right then and there,
And today I think we're a pretty good pair.
We married that I'm sure you know,
The house you built I'm proud to show.

The kids are numbered up to eight,
And this all came from our first date.
Thanks for giving me a life,
That's been so fine cause I'm your wife.

I could go on and on to say,
You're the best to me in every way.
The things you've said and the things you've done,
I'm sure you are—the only one.
That I could ever love so deep,
I hope we'll have more years to reap.

Happy 11th Anniversary 1963
My love, Toots

Chapter 2

The Spring Time of My Life

A Note to My Mom

Snow, Sunny & a Surprise every minute in our house!

Dear Folks,
   Boy—what a? I don't know what! A few quick quips from
"Lauberts' Infirmary."
   There's washing, ironing and sewing to be done, sometime
today.
   And it's half over (the day that is).
     Well, here's the score inside Laubert's door.
     uuuuuuMMMM:

Grace has the Mumps and Billy two bumps,
He fell against a window sill, then from a rocker he
did spill.

Ruth and Andy are pulling my leg, to eat in bed, they
continue to beg.

But oh dear mother, try as she does, takes the sweeper
again to pick up the fuzz.

She has washing and ironing and sewing to do.
And you can bet your life, these are only a few.

Two new machines to brighten the day, then $400 dollars
we had to pay.

One is a washer and the other a dryer.
With their help, I should be a little bit sprier.

Confirmation for Andy on Sunday,
I hope the Mumps wait till Monday.
    Love, Barbara
    March 12, 1960

zzzzZZZ   Quiet Time   ZZZzzzz

===================================

I treasure the moments of solitude,
For me there are but few.

I share with God in a peaceful mood,
The good and the bad times too.

He knows the concerns deep in my heart,
And the limits and goals of tomorrow.

He gives me the strength to finding a start,
For each precious day I can borrow.

The quiet time gives me a chance to reflect,
On the days and years gone by.

To be grateful and happy and really respect,
My HUSBAND, MY WONDERFUL Guy.

ONLY GOD COULD HAVE DONE THIS.

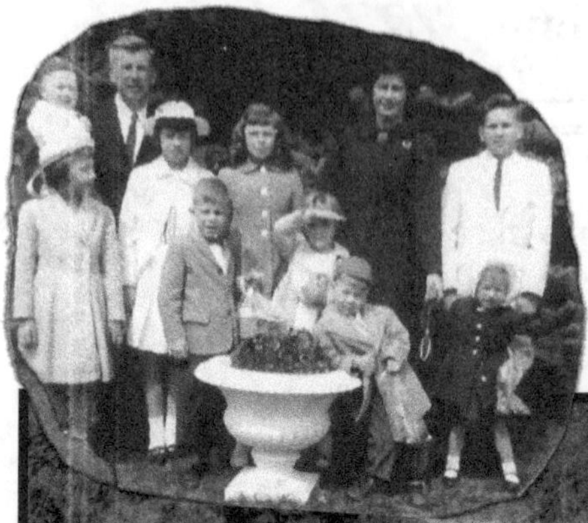

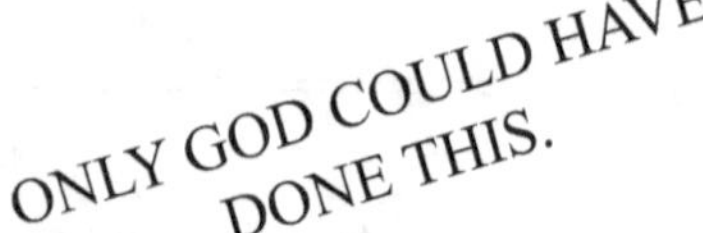

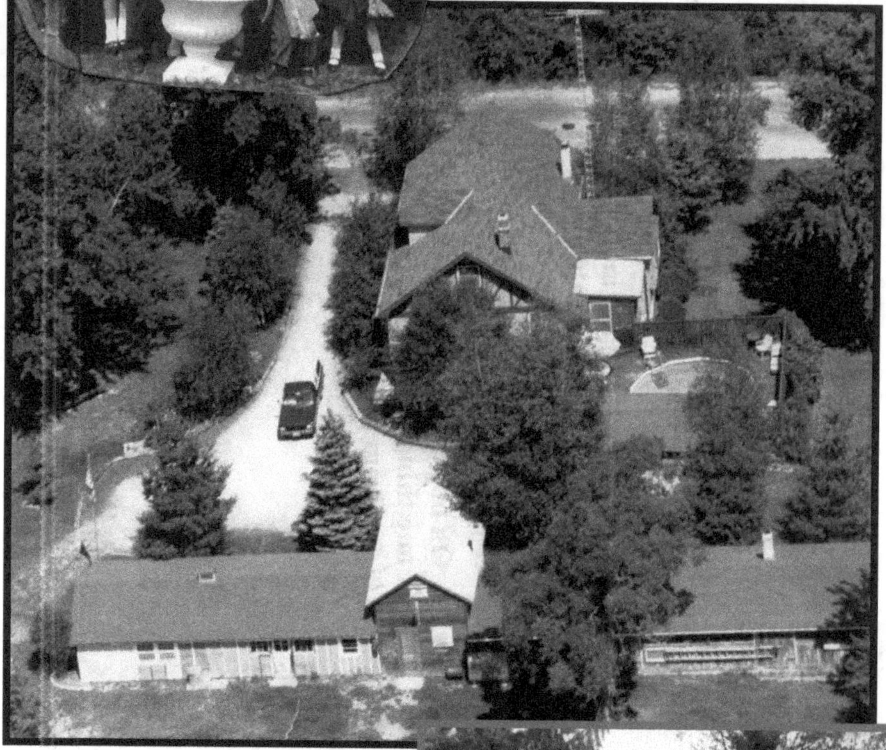

Our house before we moved South. Our third house. Andy completely added on to and remodeled the house to the right, adding a swimming pool. He converted a chicken coop to a really nice apartment -3 bedrooms, a bath, a kitchen and a living room.

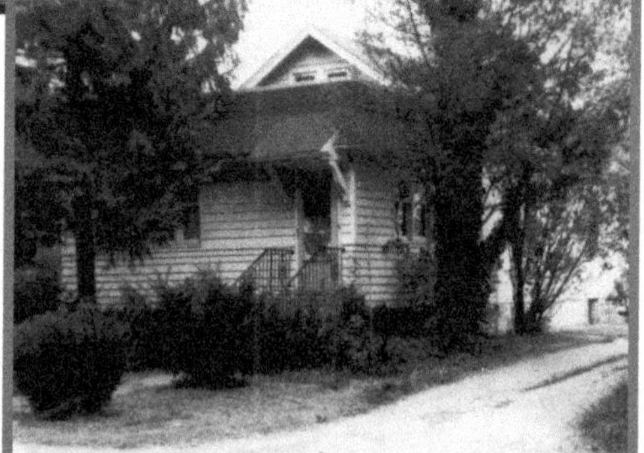

\\\\\\\\ **Broken Hearted** ////////

My heart is heavy; my body is weak,

My eyes are full; I can hardly speak.

When I think of you; my dreams just shatter,

'Cause I can't understand, what was the matter?

Love, Mom

To Lori - 1980

*****An Invitation *****

How do we say we miss you,
How do we say we care?

How do we help you realize,
The love we have to share?

The road is short—the miles are few,
We'd like to spend time with you

Dinner at 6:00, next Sunday night,
Bring Gary, and you'll enjoy a few bites.

Love, Mom
August 25, 1998, To Rosemary

============Children------------------------

CHILDREN are a challenge, which never seems to end,

It's tough to be a parent—not supposed to be a friend.

I've tried so many times and it just doesn't work,
Cause when you disagree with them, you've created only murk.

It all begins when they're very small,
It's time for a nap, they want to crawl.
Or play outside, they want to be in,
And then to bed by 8—9—or 10.

School days arrive, a schedule to keep,
Get your homework done, or you'll have to repeat.
The school bus went by, they missed it once more,
As I hollered to hurry them out of the door.

Lunch at times, they'd make such a fuss,
Then leave it behind, running after the bus.
School days soon over and done,
Now is the time when real worries begun.

To get around there's need for a car,
And to dance, well the band's at the bar.
After dancing and drinking a few,
They slinky in maybe by two.

Then there is marriage, picking a mate,
A serious matter, not just a date.
This special person committed to be,
A partner in love eternally.

GOOD HEALTH—BE TRUE—HONEST and FAIR
I'll watch from afar and always be there.

=== **Happy Valentine's Day My Love** ===

My dearest Andy, for you I live,
My love and devotion is the gift I can give.

I treasure your love and full understanding,
I hope that I'm never, much too demanding.

Our hopes and our dreams are still coming true,
So, with time and with patience, we'll make it through.

Forever yours,
Toots
(Andy's pet name for me)
February 14, 1982

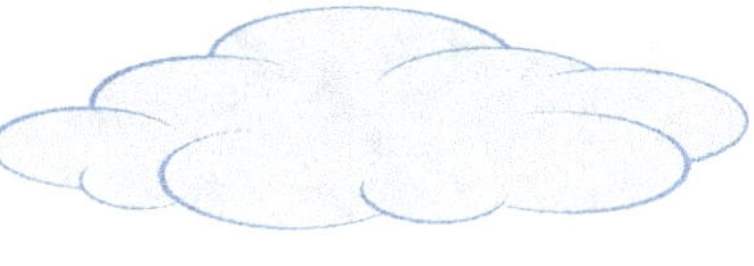

Please God

Make My days useful,

My nights restful,

My home peaceful and

my efforts fruitful.

Amen.

Our daughters wedding in 1982. I made the wedding gown and the bridesmaids' dresses.

Friends - we have so many,
Who shared a wedding day,
They brought us joy and happiness,
In such a special way.

We have no words that quite express,
The feelings down inside,
To say "Thank You" for coming,
From both far and wide,

The excitement and your presence,
Are treasures in our heart,
That are locked in tight forever,
So glad you were a part.

Goodies, gifts and lots of laughter,
Are memories now and ever after,
Should you need us - just give a yell,
Until then, God Bless and keep you well.

This was a response after Beverly and John's wedding in 1982.

)(< **Life** >)(

God blesses us with sunshine and rain,
to help all things grow.
And a partner to share life with,
A love only the two of us know.

Through struggles and triumphs,
Fulfilling our dreams,
Working together is what a great marriage means.

Now in our old age we find peace of mind,
Forgiving—forgetting, leaving troubles behind.

For now life's too short to carry the scars,
That weighed us down.
We have more smiles, and seldom a frown.

We trust YOU dear LORD, to show us the way,
We keep learning and thanking you more everyday.

We appreciate our time lived here on the earth,
Hoping our actions will be proof of our worth.

I'm holding a fork, with fingers and thumb,
For I know for sure, The best is yet to come.

By Barbara L Laubert   6-2-17

Chapter 3

Real Life Sets in the Summer of My Life

Meanest Mother in the World

I had the meanest mother in the world.
While other kids had candy for breakfast, I had to eat cereal, eggs, and toast. While other kids had cakes and candy for lunch, I had a sandwich. As you can guess, my dinner was different from other dinners too.

My mother insisted on knowing where we were at all times. You'd think we were on a chain gang or something. She had to know who our friends were and what we were doing.

I am ashamed to admit it, but she actually had the nerve to break the child labor law. That's right, She made us WORK!
We had to wash dishes, make the beds and learn how to cook. That woman must have stayed awake at nights thinking up things for us kids to do. And she insisted that we tell the truth, the whole truth and nothing but the truth.

By the time we were teenagers, she was much wiser and our life became more unbearable. None of this tooting the car horn for us to come running: she embarrassed us to no end by insisting that friends come to the door and get us.

I forgot to mention that most of our friends were allowed to date at the mature age of 12 or 13. But our old fashioned Mother refused to let us date until we were 15. She really raised a bunch of squares. None of us were ever arrested for shoplifting or busted for dope. And whom do we have to thank for this? You're right, our mean mother.

I am trying to raise my children to stand a little straighter and taller and I am secretly tickled to pieces when my children call me mean. I thank GOD for giving me the meanest Mother in the World.

Author Unknown

19 years later!!

Writing a poem has taken a long needed rest,
To find a routine for those in our nest.
Nine babies have blessed our busy life,
Diapers and bottles, I'm a warm loving wife.

A wonderful job, God filled me with joys,
Five little girls and four little boys.
Blonde hair and blue eyes made my heart sing,
In between operations that surely did sting.

Little ones cry when they trip and fall down,
Halloween came, some dressed like a clown.
School days have come, homework to be done,
A mom needs to cope, when the kids haven't begun.

I found time to write once more,
New life experiences add to the chore..
Encouraging—understanding the changes life takes,
Good and bad choices; we pray no mistakes.

'Cause life is a journey traveled far by all,
Guided by parents warning of such a pitfall.
Off to college to learn which direction to go,
Maybe changing a major that sets them aglow.

Many decisions are made everyday,
I wish for the young folks to find their way.
With the Lord's help, all things work out,
Please don't forget to, give "HIM A Shout!"

I'M WONDERING

Dear Mama,

I'm wondering—now over a year,
How a few words can cause many a tear?

I made a mistake recalling the past,
Not thinking how long conversation will last.

A real mother to me, I felt in my heart,
But now we are miles and miles apart.

In my heart the scar it still bleeds,
'Cause I thought you loved me, not only your needs.

When I see your son, changing to cold,
Toward a mama he's loved, till she's old.

I ask the good Lord, to mend both our ways,
So again we can share, those happier days.

We all have faults and I'm trying you see,
To make mine fewer, won't you help me?

1983

GREETINGS

Hello my friends, there at the bank,
The dish garden you sent is surely top rank.

I miss all you guys and even the work,
Sure hope it's not long till I'm out of this lurk.

The quilting and writing to busy my mind,
Are fun for a while to help pass the time.

But there's really something about a normal routine,
That makes you feel whole,
a real human being.

February 18, 1982
Written while in the hospital
for a blood clot in the right leg.

****

****

Thanks

Thank you for giving me a joyful stay
In Tavernier Town for many a day.

This was a big part of my 'Voyage of Love'
And I'm sure I'm protected by our God up above.

Journey on to visit my loved ones you see,
But I'll call you and share warm memories.

This was on my 4,000 mile trip in 1983.
To Lori

Dear Rosie and Don,

Let the love that you share, continue to grow,
That your children will see and sincerely know,
How God's presence—will always be,
To secure your nest, a great family.
I appreciate the love, that you shared with your mom,
Not just Rosemary—especially from Don.

The kiddies they thrill me from my head to my toes,
But when I'll get back, God only knows.
To say thank-you is easy, but good-bye is tough,
I'm not very good—about that kind of stuff.

If you ever need help or your health isn't well,
Don't be afraid, to give us a yell.
Thanks for everything, during my stay,
But now is the time—to be on my way.

Lovingly,

Mom

This was when I made my 4,000 mile trip.
"My Voyage of Love" alone to share time with,
many of my loved ones; from New Jersey
to Florida, then to Mississippi.

I had a second visit with Ruthann in Maryland on the way home.

November 12, 1983

)))))))))))))))) **Good Morning Sweetheart** (((((((((((((((((

Good morning Sweetheart,
Thank you for understanding,
The needs deep within my heart.
For now that I've traveled,
and we are miles apart.

It's a wonderful feeling,
To know that you care,
And you'll be happy to see me,
When I get back there.

I'm safe and enjoying,
My "Voyage of Love,
Cause God's watching over me,
From way up above."

Lovingly,
Toots
November 3, 1983

I know I am so selfish Lord,
To want all my kids nearby,
But they are spread so far apart,
I can't help but cry.

I pray that all their dreams come true,
But most of all, that they come to know YOU.
'Cause through the years, You've shown me how,
To be the person I am now.

I don't pretend or think I'm great,
For this I'm sure a grave mistake.
I only know that You've helped me,
Through trials and troubles as a family.

It's great—It's special and YOU know I care,
So we'll all be together, Someday,
Somewhere!

*10" x 14" charcoal drawing of Our Lord Jesus Christ done by
Babara L. Laubert in 1945 while in the Academy of Holy
Names (a boarding school for girls) in Tampa, Florida.
I was sent there for a year, due to a lung condition that needed warm
weather to make me well.*

Dear Carol and Glen,

"Thank you" is such an inadequate phrase,
Just can't find the words to cover those days.
That you cared and shared and helped me through,
Being sincere because the love shines in you.

Please accept the gratitude I try to express,
Sometime—somehow—God surely will bless
Your family and friends Carol and Glen,
I don't know how—I don't know when.,

Love, Barbara
November 1983

My 4,000 mile Trip alone!

Dear Bud and Hazel,

My visit has been a thrill, a joy and a pleasure,
Memories gained, experience too, in my heart quite a treasure,
No words can express, my thanks to you, for the welcome.
The love, hospitality—whew!!

Then Kim and Pat, together we shared,
Some laughs, good food, a family cared.
Conversations, your time is a precious gift,
You've given my life a mighty big lift.

And reading your scrapbook, how proud I can be,
Of a brother who worked so diligently.
To Hazel and Bud, plus Pat and Kim,
I'll sign off with love, yes this is the end.

November 15, 1993

Easter Egg Hunt

I'm a proud and happy mama,
To have shared some fun with you,
Just being with your family,
Thrilled me through and through.

I sure do hope the pictures—
You took of all the gang,
Turn out to be just super,
For the day was a big bang !

You know I cherish memories,
Of good times NOW and—THEN,
It seems like only yesterday,
That you were only ten.

The days and years go whizzing by,
Sometimes I wish—time didn't fly..

Love, Mom

To Andy & Roxanne
March 30, 1985

The Meaning of "LOVE"

This special little "Thank You" is to let you know I say,
"I Love You" for the joy you bring,
Into my life each day.
Words can never quite express,
The feelings way down deep,
But read my grateful message, cause
In its lines there's Love to keep.

My Thoughts about the meaning of:

      L—lasting (permanent)
      O—omnipotent (unlimited power)
      V—voluntary (exercise of one's own free will)
      E—eternal (forever the same)

Omni—A—VIN—CIT—AMOR

LOVE overcomes all (THINGS)

1982

This Little Box

We send our love in this little box
Imagine it's like powder,
So fine and pure—goes everywhere,
We can't say it any louder.

The dust it soothes our rough spots,
And helps us to cool down,
It lays a film on tender skin,
It takes away our frown.

The particles are spread—Both from here to there,
In hopes the love we send,
You'll welcome with our care.

****
****

zzzzzzzzzzzzzz My Comfy zzzzzzzzzzzzzzz

Two minutes in the microwave,
Will warm me just enough,

To take away your aches and pains,
Those hurts that are so tough.

On ear, elbow, neck and hand,
You'll find my "Comfy" in demand.

This is a rice bag that I made and sold many.

This young bride saw my Beverly's wedding gown in the window of our Grace's store. She stopped by to ask if I would make her a wedding gown just like the one in the window. I did make her gown and then all of her bridesmaid's.

About 1985!

Showboat's Christmas

Christmas is coming and at Showboat there'll be,
Garland with ornaments on many a tree.

A beautiful sight to bring joy for us all,
The happiest feelings will fill our hall.

I've been at Showboat now well past a year,
I wish I had known that this job was here.

There's always some fun mixed in with the work,
Being with young people, sure helps you perk.

On birthdays there's cake and farewells a party,
And most often than not, no one is tardy.

We all get along unusually well,
We're waiting to hear the Christmas bell.

Holiday carols through the casino are heard,
This is the season when magic occurs.

So come join the fun at the tables of chance,
If you make a winning, you'll want to dance.

Then dine in the restaurants, or stay the night,
I'm sure you will leave with memories of delight.

Happy Birthday Barbara!
Enjoy—a blast from our past at Showboat.

Put in the Wedding Bible

This Bible is given to you,
Bill and Barbara C. Laubert

With the Faith, that you can Trust
each other Forever.

The Hope, that you build a strong future,

and you have the Love to sustain,

The many trials of life.

Our love always,
Mom & Dad

March 15, 2001

Chapter 4

**After Moving South
in the Fall of My Life**

Over The Years I Found Peace

>>>>>>>>>>>>>>>>>>>>>>>>>>

I have a man, who's just right for me,
He has hugs and kisses and fills me with glee,
I need to express, all the love, that's inside,
So happy I took him for that very first ride.

I appreciate how well he's taken care of me,
Plus our nine kids, it's been quite a journey!
He's always provided a safe car,
So I could travel, no matter how far.

Over the years he continues to build,
His work should be in the builder's guild.
One home after another, work on as he does,
Making us happy, sure gives us a buzz.

Often he'll bring me a sweet little gift,
Showing his love always gives me a lift.
My man, he's still working at eighty-six,
People are asking about things to be fixed.

Oh how I love this guy, with so many talents,
But it's the checkbook that won't balance.
From the day we met, 'til I was his bride,
For 65 years now, by each other's side.

Beverly—big question?
I can't figure out,
No communication, what's it all about?
Douglas—so thoughtful, so loving, so dear,
What has happened?
These last few years?

Good example?
Choices?
Some stay—some stray.

Life is a daydream,
That doesn't work out,
The way that you thought,
And dreamed all about!

))))))))))))))) ooooooooooo (((((((((((((((((

Our move south created much dis-content!

My hubby and I moved from New Jersey in 1993.
We have nine children—5 girls and 4 boys:
all were born in eleven years, plus 1 miscarriage.
This was a huge job to raise my babes to respect others, be truthful,
honest, loving, fair and oh so much more. I did my best.
Our youngest adult was 30 years old when we moved. So my
mindset was that, three of our girls were scattered around the USA,
and the boys were settled into their jobs to make lives of their own.
In Georgia there were two daughters and their new families,
which we only had been able to see maybe once a year.
Lexington, Georgia is where we settled—1026 known as
"Paradise Found," a wonderful place to come visit.
Needless to say—our young adults up north have been quite upset.
I followed my man, so this was our decision. We love it here! Just me!

Dear One, These letters mean so much to me,
I've kept them safe for your memories.
Read them over and recollect,
Old times and places, just reflect.

Good decisions—some bad,
Lots of fun—sometimes sad,
Wishes never end—and attitudes bend,
Many strangers—very few true friends.

Time flies—we're getting old,
The letters will help with stories told.
My love continues, whether near or far,
Please remember my door—is always ajar.

We toured this castle, "Neuschwanstein," which is the castle that Disney World copied to build in Florida. One of the absolutely greatest experiences we have ever had! Just imagine living back in those days!

Fortunately, we have pictures to reflect on those wonderful trips.

The huge house in the picture on the previous page is actually a working Cuckoo clock with very large gears in action inside the building. This working clock also has a window on the upper outside that opens and cuckoos on the hour. So many wonderful memories!

Siggy was our foreign exchange student friom Germany in 1969. He lived with us for almost a year. A young man we truly enjoyed. Siggy fit right in with our family of nine children. 30 years later he invited us to visit Germany for 3 weeks where he toured us all over Germany. A second trip was a two week trip with more touring all around West Germany. Five years after that, in Austria we had the opportunity to experience the carvers at work. And then Oberamagau theater shows the (Passion Play) which is only performed once every 10 years.

My Child

I brought you up with LOVE, PRAISE and COMMITMENT.

To build within you, Personality, Character, and Self-esteem.
That you strive for Wholesome Accomplishments.

To be Honest and Fair—with Dignity.
Showing others Compassion, Love and Understanding.

To Honor the LORD and Live by HIS Commandments.
All this will Guard you against the Temptations of EVIL,
Immorality or Corruption.

Then pass all your Goodness on to your children and then theirs.

I look forward to growing old enough to witness,

All these things, knowing then,

That I've done my job, as a MOM.

December 1996

Mother Cries Out 

Yes, me~~I do cry out~~with my eyes WIDE OPEN~~and someday my eyes will be WIDE SHUT!

I'm so happy your dad brought us to Georgia. Here we've found a peace.
After years of building what I wanted, "A Family,"
Giving all we had - of ourselves to make you good people.

Never going on expensive trips, or even out to dinner to any of those fabulous places that seem so necessary today. [I mean with MOM - DAD & KIDS].
You know, a special vacation. I wish we could have done these things as a family. They just didn't fit into our budget.

Going to church on Sundays - hoping you'd learn about our awesome GOD and caring for our parents - our bills - your teeth - a nice warm home - and a reliable car, that you were safe in. Keeping food on the table and then enjoying Sunday dinners together when you were old enough to fly the nest.

All these were signs of our LOVE - hoping to bind us into a STRONG - HEALTHY - HAPPY - family. I guess it wasn't enough?

It's been six years since we left New Jersey. I see today, some of the mistakes we made. Yes, I'm tortured!!

No laughs from our boys - No dinners - Really - NOBODY borrows this or that - Never did go shopping with my girls - Still miss that. The problems to FACE are much less down here. We have A PEACE.

Your daddy's health is 100% better and my nerves are too. But our hearts are HEAVY, cause the closeness of our WONDERFUL KIDS is so darned empty. We gave you each other - Help and care about each other, I hope that's important. Have a get together once a month or so!

And one day - My eyes will be WIDE SHUT.

March 1999

((((((((((**I LOVE YOU**   ))))))))))

As I sit back and reminisce
Of years when you were small,
My heart fills with warm and loving times,
I tried to cuddle all.

Building rockets, digging worms,
And a tree house to the sky,
Dressing up to give a show,
The laughter makes us cry.

Great big milk cans, laundry chutes,
And donkey rides to share,
The playhouse, barn, and cave-like dens,
Sometimes gave us a scare.

Broken bones, sewn-up cuts,
And falling from a tree,
Kids sure do cause for worry,
Es–pec–ial–ly for me.

We have five girls and four boys,
I made clothes—Dad made toys,
My babies are my dreams come true,
I hope you know that I Love YOU.

June 8, 1999

Andy's mother, Rose

(((((((((((((((((Things Shared)))))))))))))))))
(Remembering With Love)

As I look around my home and see,
Items that have been given to me,
I realize all the love that's been shared.

The bedroom radiates Grandma's wise choice,
With dignity and soft manner of voice.
Aunt Eleanor's desk, where debts, are paid on time,
A footstool and chair, are favorites of mine

Mama Laubert added a daybed and so,
There's a place to rest or maybe doze.
Coffee table and sofa, the Steelmans were kind,
Where guests can sleep if they don't mind.

Grandma and Granddad's lamps shed the light,
To keep our den and living room bright.
Daughter Gracie provided a glass cabinet to view,
My dolls, of which there's more than a few.

Mom's sewing machine gets used Oh so much,
Where I mend or create dresses and such.
Mrs. Klock supplied the oak sewing chest,
To hold fabric and patterns, etcetera the best.

So many more things are around our home,
My heart swells with joy, just thinking alone.
I cherish all of these gifts sharing love,
Especially Nan's Bible, with guidance from above.

Thanks to all who have contributed a share,
To make our house a home, I AM AWARE.

October 17, 2000

Oh Gracie, we love you, where else can I start!
It's just plain awful to be far apart.
We send you warm hugs, to help hold you together,
Why don't you come south, we're having warm weather?

We have nothing to offer but love and care,
But it's real and honest, and we have lots to share.
We want you to know you're welcome in our home,
When you make up your mind, to let the devil alone.

He's corrupted your body, your mind, and your soul,
And it's left in our hearts a mighty big hole.
We'll patiently wait, till the LORD wiggles in,
To your heart and your soul, to release you from sin.

He'll do it we know, for we've not been let down,
The proof Gracie will be when you come into town.
To join us again ~ MOM & DAD can wait,
For that Wonderful ~ Glorious ~ Marvelous Date.

September 23, 2001

About 2010 we were part of the Senior Olympics that took place in Warner Robbins, Georgia. Each year there's a new theme for the Dinner Dance.

"The Best Dressed Couple," Andy and I took "first place."

>>>>>>>>>>> **Christmas Greetings** <<<<<<<<<<<<

I have a list of folks I know, all written in a book,
And every year at Christmas time I go and look.
And that is when I realize that these names are a part,
Not of the book they're written in, but of my very heart.

Each name stands for someone whose path
touched mineand then,
Left such a print of friendship that I want to touch again.
And while it sounds fantastic for me to make this claim,
I really feel I composed of each remembered name.

And while you may not be aware of any special link,
Just meeting you has shaped my life more than you might think.
For once you've met somebody, the years cannot erase,
The memory of a pleasant word or of a friendly face.

So never think my Christmas cards are just a mere routine,
Of names upon a Christmas card that is addressed to you,
It's because you're on that list of folks I am indebted to.

For one is but a total of the many folks they've met,
And you happen to be one of those I prefer NOT to forget.
And whether I have known you for many years or few.
In some way you have had a part in shaping things I do.

And every year when Christmas comes, I realize anew.
THE BIGGEST GIFT life can give is
MEETING FOLKS LIKE YOU.

And may the Spirit of Christmas that forever and ever endures,
Leave its richest blessings in the hearts of YOU and YOURS.

MERRY CHRISTMAS

(*)(*)(******)(**In Strength I Grow**)(*****)(*)(*)

Oh, dear GOD, through YOU I grow,
In strength, in faith, I hope it shows.
My prayers go forth to share the love,
Of family on earth, to radiate above.

Keep all my loved ones safe today,
Wiggle into their hearts in a special way.

Guide them through their daily chores,
Open up some opportune doors.
That we all can have the joys of life,
Yet keep YOU close, avoiding strife.

Yes, dear LORD, some have strayed,
Others serve you; they have stayed.
My prayers continue, with hope secure,
In YOUR time LORD, all things sure.

I have a son who is walking proof,
Of YOUR never ending - love aloof.
You've made me strong in heart and mind,
I'll endure the pains - of our mankind.

September 24, 2001

!!!! Sadness ~~~ oh, such sadness!!!! (tears) !!! (tears)
Our family is lacking glue, stick-to-itiveness! ~~
Where have we gone wrong?

Is working hard to keep our surroundings clean, neat and
Attractive ~~ a mistake?
Or cooking, washing clothes, sewing, and teaching manners.
The drawback to making a family stick?

How about religion? And setting a good example?
My dreams have been shattered; I feel empty.
Why do we continue to have a nice home?
Happy meals ~ and clean beds?

Or enjoy decent friends?
To speak kindly towards each other?
Many times, I've wished my own tongue would be cut out!
I have expressed sarcasm and hurt as a defense.

When I feel I am right, or I am being attacked.
When you try so hard to be close with your kids,
Why are you so far apart and want to give up?
This is a mystery to me.

My thoughts are with Jesus,
Yes, He is my strength,
My TRUST in Jesus will carry me through,
To the gates of heaven ~ nothing else I can do!

############### **BRIDGES** ###############

Doug, I know you're turning 40,
Miss you, miss you—Yes, Oh Lordy,
Life makes changes we can't explain,
Sometimes they cause, a lot of pain.

Some are those we don't expect,
Understanding comes with due respect.
This applies to both you and me,
Let us bridge this troubled sea.

I think about you, Oh so much,
That's why I wish we'd keep in touch.
I love you more than words can say,
You're on my mind everyday.

I hear your voice, your love, your care,
I have memories of you everywhere.
The pleasure's mine to hear you sing,
And being funny, is a gift you bring.

Your talents are so bright and strong,
Wish I could change what ere went wrong.
Visit or write—a phone call will do,
Life's too short to be without you.

My loving son, for you to know,
This poem I write, for my LOVE to show.

Happy Birthday!
Love, Mom

May 16, 2001

This is Douglas

No. 7 adult of our 9 children

Doug came to live with us 10 years ago.
A bachelor who struggles with Diabetes
and several other problems.
We've taken care of him and now he takes
care of us. At 61 years old he does a great
job to be there for ALL of our necessities.
Special THANKS Douglas!

Love, Mom & Dad

On June 23, 2013 my son Douglas gave me this 1963 Rambler Convertible. I was totally shocked, surprised and happy.

Boy, did he bring back memories!

My Mama Used To...

**My mama used to sing to me two little songs I'll never forget.
One went like this:**

I had a little puppy, skinny as a rail,
He had no head or feet, and such a stubby tail.
He didn't bite, he didn't bark or even jump around,
You bought him in a butcher shop,
For fifty cents a pound.
Hot Dog!

And the other talked about women on bicycles
In the vinter time, in the summertime,
Vhen the vind, blows around the vindow pane,
Vhen the vimen in the vaudeville,
Ride velocipedes in the vestibule.

Oh boy!
Grammy and Grandpop!
What a day!
I am so excited,
I do not know what to say!
Two wonderful people,

Related to me,
Oh what a fun day,
This is going to be!

They are so fun,
They are so sweet,
To have them here,
Boy, what a treat!

I LOVE YOU BOTH!!!!!!!!!

*Written by my Granddaughter,
Michelle Puleo Age 14*

No More Tears

>>>>>>>>>>>>>>>>>>>

Our Gracie dear, "No More Tears."
It's been now, over twenty years.
Your children love you, can't you see?
What a wonderful SON, a fine man is he!
Still caring enough to raise your kids,
Only his love, could take the jibs......
His wife by his side, a really tough job.
Mothering your kids—her own babes she robs.

Young George is one, who's experienced shock,
His life was crushed, by a huge falling rock.
Him loosing a Dad and you loosing a mate,
A page remembered in the book of fate.

Then your daughters "all three,"
Have been there to help, cook and wash—oh me!
Angry, unhappy, disturbed and distraught,
Remain strong in HOPE, your health can be brought,
Back to NORMAL—as your life started out,
So we all "someday" will be happy to shout.

Yes, Gracie, you are loved by more than a few,
Give GOD a chance, He'll help you through.
Avoiding temptation, bad company and sin.
To grow warm and content and no anger within.
Oh Gracie, I said, "No More Tears.
But, they just keep coming, over the years.
You know we all love you and want you to be,
The MOM, daughter and friend "you were when you're free.

Lovingly, Mom
August 20, 2021

Our hands, they toiled to keep you warm,
Our hearts, with LOVE so bold.

Our eyes saw all the good in you,
Our arms, super hugs did hold.

Now let these photos bring to mind,
Who nurtured you with care.

Knowing we're your mom and dad,
And surely always there.

Lovingly,
Mom & Dad

Andy and Barbara's hands

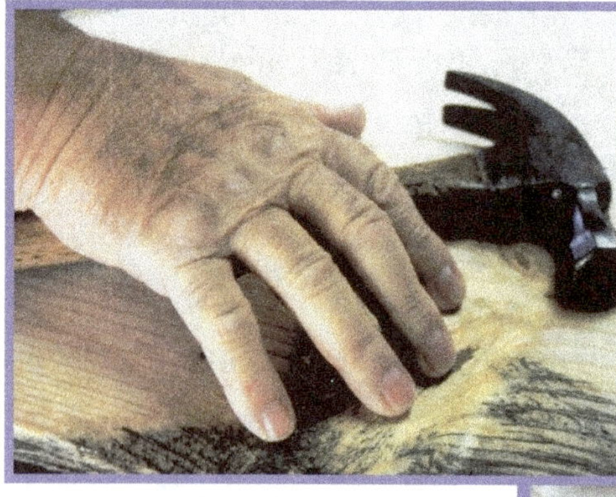

This poem is on the back of framed photos of Andy's and Barbara's hands. Merry Christmas, 2001.

<u>///</u>
<u>_OOOOOOOOOOOO_</u>

Dear Gracie ~~ You're special!!! Surely God knows,
What a tough road and so many blows.
We talk of a tunnel with a light at the end,
You're on the journey and rounding the bend.

The family you love and want to unite,
Is waiting on that road, don't give up the fight.
Our hearts are so lifted, seeing you begin,
Back to a mom, who can make dinners again.

Cleaning and painting and laughing, Oh Boy!
I just cannot tell you, what a wonderful joy!
The light's getting brighter and work has begun.
You'll make it my dear, hopes and dreams can be fun.

Think of the good times and make future plans.
Then you'll see your efforts, fill in your demands.
Our prayers will continue till you've accomplished your goal.
Let the past be gone, no longer taking its toll.

Your loving mom, XXOO unconditionally!

<u>_OOOOOOOOOOOO_</u>
<u>_OOOOOOOOOOOO_//_OOOOOOOOOOOO_</u>

Prayer of Forgiveness

OOOOOOOOOOOOOOOOOOO
OOOOOOOOOOO///OOOOOOOOOOO

Dear Lord,
If I am wrong, right me,
If I'm lost, guide me.
If I start to give up,
Please keep me going,
Lead me in light and love.

Amen

I made this seed bead arrangement as a memorial of our 50th Wedding Anniversary.

########## **Beads of Love** ##########

==

Beads of love, I thread with care.
Cedar bases by dad are hewn to share.
The token for memories you've sent our way,
Those many years past ~ new ones today.

From bottles to diapers and pins and such,
Then teenagers, adults, now parents in touch.
It's your turn to guide, to teach and to show,
Whatever you learned and want yours to know.

Life's road is still changing, we take a new bend,
A whirlwind of busy that just doesn't end.
What a pleasure it's been, to share life with you,
Thanks for the love that radiates through.

Driving and flying ~ to both far and wide,
Sharing a meal, a joke, a goodbye.
Lots of fun, work and joy, sometimes a tear,
Most of all ~ remember ~ Mom & Dad are near!

December 7, 2002

*********Thank You for Christmas*** 2002 *****

Holidays over and the excitement winds down,
We've been very busy,
With some time out of town.

We need to say thank you right from our heart,
For your visit—your card—your gift.
It all made this season the happiest part.

"Beads of Love"—this year's endeavor,
The base—the globe—and the flowers,
Showing we care is beyond any measure.

Time slips away when involved as we are,
With making our gifts,
For those near and far.

There were cards that now would be oh so late,
So, we send this with love,
To make up for that date.

Our grateful thanks,
Mom and Dad

January 9, 2003

Letter to Ellie

Dear Ellie,
    Happy Birthday my old friend of long ago,
A red headed girl from Naylor's Run Road,
We played Indian Ball on the side of my house,
And a miniature store and paper dolls at yours.
Kick the can was a game we played in the street,
There were lots of kids on the block
We lived about 4 houses apart along the creek.
Together we walked to school each day.
Across the big pipe, that crossed the creek.
Through somebody's yard and then the railroad tracks.
Llanerch School is where we went—1-6 grade.
Remember the candy store across from the school?

    Then Haverford High—we were growing up.
The school was HUGE! We all got lost at first.
And only 20 minutes for lunch—darn.
Halloween was so much fun. I remember carrying
A pillowcase to fill with goodies.
Just going around the block gave us enough to make
Us sick. Many, many kids all lived close by.
How about swimming in the creek in the summer

    Then trying to skate on the ice in winter.
We were so lucky to have lived back then.
We were innocent, curious and had no responsibilities.
WWII was on—rationing of food and gas,
Mom made margarine out of a yellow ball and
Some white stuff, to take the place of butter.
People were trading stamps to help each other.

Dads needed gas stamps and moms needed them for food.
Kids would save 10cent war bond stamps in a book,
When the book was full it would buy a war bond.
But as kids we really didn't realize, how everybody
Helped and sacrificed, during the war.
Remember too, how all the houses on our street
Looked alike, but painted different ways.
Our mamas had coffee klach and kuken (together & cake)
They were really nice homes and so many good neighbors.

Well, my dear friend, I hope this has brightened your day.
Have a Happy Birthday with love and good health,

An old pal,
Barbara Wilson Laubert

^^^^^^^^^ **For My Honey** ^^^^^^^^^

Today ~ is the day I met you.
One I'm grateful for,
Cause life's been mighty good to me,
We're not rich and surely not poor.

You thrill me with Rose buds,
Gentle squeezes and such,
I'll love you forever,
Cause I enjoy your tender touch.

Your humor makes me smile,
And we laugh together on a whim.
Through years and all those trials,
Many bruises on the chin.

Now here we are in Georgia,
Hills of "Paradise Found,"
A garden, shop and concrete blocks,
Make our home on an acre of ground.

Cuckoo clocks and Angel pup,
Talk to us all day,
Both need our close attention,
In their own very special way.

Our shape and looks have changed a lot,
But our love remains the same.
To have and to hold ~ forever more,
Is the goal, we forge on to obtain.

Love, Toots,
Written on August 14, 2000
about August 14, 1951

* * * * **While Waiting** * * * *

I sit here and wait
for the hour to pass,
While Andy works out in his Cardiac class.
The time goes by quickly with writing to do,
Jotting down thoughts that come out of the blue.

Thirty minutes of walking to strengthen the heart,
Loose weight—eat right—is a good place to start.
Fifty four years now since we were wed,
Learning new foods we're supposed to be fed.

Each of us different in so many ways,
Yet we've become 1 - for the rest of our days.
Living with hope for a great many more,
To experience the joys we daily explore.

Our nine children have charted their course,
Some have been steady and some have divorced.
Well, time's up, Andy's class came to an end,
We look forward to life turning a bend.

2006

I Miss You

I wish I could find the words to express,
The reasons for moving and not cause distress.
I'll never know if it's right or it's wrong,
I only know that I need to be strong.

For a mom and dad's love, to spread and to share,
No matter how old they get, never stopping the care.
As each one in our nest has a niche in my heart,
Cause they were wanted and loved, right from the
start.

Life is a daydream that doesn't work out,
The way you expected or thought all about.
I thank God we don't know what is in store,
For we'd never keep going, to live on for more.

But finding the Lord along the way,
Is the answer to living from day to day.
Cause life with a purpose, to meet Jesus again,
Is a beautiful thought and a wonderful end.
Since life everlasting is His great Promise,
To be with OUR LOVED ONES, those that we miss.

Love, Mom and Dad

1993

((((((((((((((**A Box of Tissues**   ))))))))))))))

Tissues are a comfort to wipe away the tears,
That come from all the happy times we share o'er all the years.
First the joy of giving birth, our babies small and pink,
Then watching as they grow and discover how to think.
I was so blessed ~ God gave me nine ~
All babies were born ~ physically fine.

The years go by ~ oh so fast,
Sometimes we wish young years would last.
Off to school with other kids, brothers and sisters too,
Tears they come ~ THE TISSUES ~ for runny noses will ensue.
Scrapes and bruises along the way,
Tomorrow will be a better day.
Kindergarten thru twelve, over and done ~
More tears of joy, adult life has begun.

A car, college and then a career,
All these decisions bring many a tear.
Then finding a mate ~ somewhere in the crowd,
Someone you trust ~ who will make you so proud.
Those tissues are soft, to dry your face,
Offered by mom, with a gentle embrace.
Who knew these kids would bring such joys?
Some were girls ~ and some were boys.

Twenty Grands my heart holds dear,
And they are bringing MORE babes ~ year after year.
Fifteen Greats we have up 'till now,
Please, loved ones ~ I'll take the bow.
Here I am ~ at age 74 ~
My dreams came true ~ God blessed me more.

I am so happy ~ the tears do flow,
Give me a TISSUE, for my nose to blow.
Being a MOM brings so much pleasure,
The memories remain, a lifelong treasure.

Happy Mother's Day!

May 13, 2007

Front Row: Gracie, Beverly, Lori, Ruthann
Back Row: Gregory, Douglas, Rosemary, Bill and Andy, Jr.

///***///*** The Joys of a Mother ***///***///

The moment you learn you'll be bearing a child,
The thrill of a wiggle or turn,
With the very first cry, a giggle or smile,
Countless joys before long you will learn.
To hold and caress, this warm helpless gift,
Is a feeling hard to explain!
The miracle of life, gives you a lift,
After enduring those hours of pain.

A baby's soft skin, sweet smell and touch,
Brings feelings of a warm gentle glow.
Diapers and bottles, tiny clothes and such,
Things needed when little ones grow.
Holding on to my fingers the baby can stand,
With the trust and assurance of Mom,
Uncertain, dependent, squeezing my hand,
Tiny fingers are white, nearly numb.

First teeth, crawling, then maybe a step,
Are milestones that mark an event.
Talking, then school. How proud ~ I wept.
Many hours of homework are spent.
A family grows ~ bringing more joys,
Around the dining room table.
Suppertime laughter, 5 girls and 4 boys,
Are memories I frequently label.

Driving to drama, sports and much more,
Dating ~ a ballgame ~ a play,
Waiting and praying till you hear the door.
The end of another day!
Engagements and weddings, invitations to make,

Sewing and planning go into action.
When the day comes and they're cutting the cake,
The bride and groom are the main attraction.

    They are men and women for which I am proud,
With their heads on straight and doing well.
I feel inner peace ~ enjoying the crowd,
In my heart and soul, do tell.
Knowing the joys that come with time,
Grand-babies and travel, both far and wide.
To know all the offspring from children of mine,
Is a MOTHER'S most wonderful pride.

I can't figure out why it is ~
A mom and dad spend at least 20 years,
Building a family,
A great ~ and a good one too!
In our hearts ~ it was our future,
A dream come true.

But then our seedlings grow up,
To seek lives of their own,
Get busy with new family,
With no time to roam.

Can't see them everyday,
Like when they were a child,
Would feel good to squeeze,
Only once in a while.

Very few phone calls,
And letters don't come,
It's really upsetting,
We feel pretty bummed.

We miss having dinners,
And a shoulder to lean on,
Both now and ever after,
We'll adjust one by one.

We miss all our kids ~ all of them,
Not one, two or three,
Cause they're all extra special,
Especially ~ to ME!!

My love to you,   Mom

Sorry guys ~ this is how I feel!
I followed my man ~ your DAD ~ as
he followed me years ago!

<ins>*!!!!! Brother Bill   !!!!!*</ins>

<ins>*Dear Bill,*</ins>
I don't think you know me,
I know I don't know you.
But maybe thru some emails,
We could bring about anew?

We can share your childhood stories,
And rekindle that old love;
For I cherish you my brother,
God sent you from above.

The tools given to you from our Dad,
You've shared with our son Bill.
He'll treasure them forever,
Such an everlasting thrill.

Although you're many miles away,
And we hardly ever speak,
I hope some day we bridge the gap,
Before we get too weak.

An apology for all shortcomings,
And here's love to warm your heart,
You're a gem that lasts forever,
I knew it from the start.

HAPPY BIRTHDAY!

Love, Barbara & Andy
April 22, 2009

****Thanksgiving**** Thanks for the Roof ****

Thank you my son, for getting the crew,
Re-roofing our porch, in a day or two.
There was Stephen, young Steve and George,
John, Sean and Max and Douglas of course.

You all worked together, so fast and strong,
The old roof off and nothing went wrong.
Bud and Kim were sweeping debris,
Keeping the steps to the house dirt free.

Repairs were made; new wood was put down,
Tar paper and shingles; the color was brown.
No more wet spots or damage will be,
No more worries of what next will we see.

You all did such a fabulous job,
So good in fact, you made us sob.
You all came—from so far away,
A heck of a thought, for a holiday!

We treasure your love and willingness to help,
These two old folks who let out a yelp!
All this was followed by Thanksgiving fare,
A turkey and ham with the fix~in's to share...

Lori made Cheesecake and Ruthann Pumpkin pies,
Our gathering enriched our fast moving lives.
Twenty-four in all around the table so big,
Enjoying each other and stuffed like a pig!

Oh, how we love you, every single one,
We ate and laughed and had so much fun.
"The Bag" was a blast, a whole years collection.
Of stuff you can use or maybe rejection.

The game a tradition from many years past,
Enhances the season with memories that last.
I'd like to mention all those who joined us that Thanksgiving.
Nov 26, 2009

Uncle Bub Wilson and cousin Kim Wilson Daum
John, Beverly, Max, Sean and Sophia Fineran
Ruthann Laubert Donaldson and Douglas Laubert
Stephen Jr., Toni, Stephen III, Lindsey Michel and George Perona
Rick, Lori, Amy, Emily Glinkski and Camille Davenport
John and Hannah Puleo

Thank you for all coming to celebrate our wonderful holiday!!!
Love, Mom & Dad / Gram and Pop

For Unto us a Child is Born…Unto us a Son is Given…

Christmas is coming. A birthday for Jesus, giving gifts and goodies that surely do please us. To family and friends from our dear Lord
above, sending them wishes of our sincere love. Andy and I are delighted to share, memories gone by to make you aware. Our family now
numbers a big 61, still counting, my gosh, what have we begun?

2009 has quickly flown by, but I'll try to remember the trips we did
fly. Off to New Jersey to visit our crew, we met Bernie, Aidan, Ronan
and Andrew. Beverly, John, Max, Sean and Soph, then Billy and Barb
to go see their boat. Doug always gives us a funny show, we can't help
but laugh at his jokes, you know. Greg, Gay and Meredith always find
time, to catch us up with what's on their mind.

February a journey to Miami we flew, Carol, her parents whom
we long ago knew. Brother Bill's reunion and their children so dear—
caused for such joy and many a tear.

In the Caribbean—to Nassau and Key West, five days on a cruise
ship—we had a good rest. Except for the last night—I injured my knee.
At home—to the doctor, then surgery. Doug came south with a mechan-
ical chair, home only a while for my knee to repair. What a big help the
chair proved to be, lifting me gently and setting me free.

Oh yes, in June I could wait no longer, to see our kids—only grew
stronger. Ruthann arranged for a 10-day jaunt, Mississippi, New Jersey
and Texas we flit. Our kids in New Jersey gave us a party, with friends
and loved ones; we all ate hardy. Nancy and Lois met me for lunch, at
Fred and Ethel's, on salads we munched.

From there to Mississippi we flew, my brother Bud and Kim were
there too. New restaurants and Hudson's we try, always looking—for
an extra good buy. The casinos are fun, no money to win, but once in a
while we let the wheels spin.

Off to Houston where Ruthann resides—Andy works on the jobs—
that she decides. Over the years Ruthann has worked hard, remodeling

her home and taking care of her yard. Not many girls would tackle such a task—she makes us proud to see work that will last.

And now I'm bound to a far-off land, it's Ireland I'll see with one of our clan. Yes, Bernie, Aidan, Ronan and me, had three weeks of fun with her great family. To the Fairy Tree, Dolmans, and parties we went, the zoo, castles and ferry-ride event. Visiting relatives so warm and sincere, these memories I shall forever hold dear.

In October we went to New Jersey again, our prayers were answered, yes it was God's plan. The airport to Bev's—is about 2 hours, our Andy and family with kindness they shower. They put us up for a day or two, then drive us south to have fun with our crew. Evenings at Bev's, where the family gathers, just being together, is what truly matters.

September 29th I flew to Rochester, NY for a week's visit with my friend of 66 years, Joanie Barlow. She was a bridesmaid in my wedding nearly 64 years ago. We have fun going to yard sales, consignment shops, and she has enjoyable friends who share laughs and good times with me too. I met Francis, a bubbly gal from Poland. She treated us to some home-made Pierogis and other great pastry. We had many special treats along with reminiscing about years when we were just kids. I also enjoyed the lessons at her church, where I also met other fine friends. The minister is a powerful speaker, who was also very friendly. Just about every night we did our share of playing Canasta.

Joanie shares her beautiful clothes with me year after year. I don't like to shop, so Joanie saves me that way too! The week went way too fast!

During November we had several doctor visits, all due to aging. On the whole, we are doing just fine. Still able to travel some and living without assistance. Can't hear and the eyes are working OK. Arthritis— Oh yeah, but what the heck, we have pills for that. Dr. Das says he'll take care of us so we can see 100—Ha! At any rate no serious complaints.

Here we are in December. Just got home from a 10-day trip to New Jersey. To say the least—we were exhausted. We both slept for two days. I mean really, 2 days! Our trip North was busy with a fine lunch at Nancy's and Helen was there too. Nancy helped me out by giving me a crochet hook so I could make a "Cat Hat" for Sophie's cat. This was the first time we were able to share a birthday with Sophie who is already 10 years old. She is Beverly and John's surprise little girl. She's 12 years younger than Sean or 14 years younger than Max! Surprise!

Here's a little story about Sophie:
During the week Bevy and John thought that Sophie would have fun decorating the tree. Sophie would have fun decorating the Christmas tree with me (her Grammy). Well, Sophie and I started decorating—only about 15 minutes went by and she lost interest. Time went by—no Sophie—so John and I finished decorating the tree. Unbeknownst to me, Sophie was upset that we didn't wait for her to decorate. She told her dad that she was going to undress the tree. Lo and behold, when I got up the next morning I came downstairs and the tree was absolutely bare. Sophie completely stripped the whole tree! I was dumbfounded! John said OK—now you have to decorate the tree by yourself—and she did it her way!

Our adopted (lots of love) Dave and Pam—our niece—had us feast on dinner that was super, with all the fixings! Then a variety of desserts that was also scrumptious.

I must mention that upon our arrival we experienced the most beautiful scene. Dave had Christmas lights around every window—doorway—the entire house was outlined with lights. Lights were all the way down the driveway, around his gym and the rec room building too. By the way, Dave built his own Log Cabin and one for his mom next door to his home. And recently discovered his talent using a chainsaw to carve animals out of logs and branches. There must have been 100+ carvings in his front yard, with lights to show them off. A real craftsman and a guy we're happy to call our son. Pam, please don't feel slighted, if it wasn't for you finding Dave we couldn't say all of these nice things. You and Dave are a special couple. Love you both.

Nieces Joann and Flossie with their mother Bertha (Andy's sister) were in the dinner party. It has been 23 years since Andy and Bertha had seen each other. It was good to make amends and we all enjoyed conversation, good food and listening to Dave sing while playing the guitar.

Dave's friend Dave Costello was there too, who I had a special talk about what he's been doing with his life. Our best remembrance about Dave C. was when he wore a Gorilla suit to perform in the casino. We returned to Paradise Found on December 16th, eight days before Christmas. I plan on having the Christmas dinner at our house, with at least 12 guests to celebrate the birth of our Lord Jesus Christ. Again, the Lord gives us the opportunity to celebrate as a family in his honor.

A wonderful stay at Doug's Mill Estate, but the rain didn't stop for eight days straight. Greg was quite busy but he kept in touch, dinner with loved ones, we enjoyed so much. We saw Mere's pictures and musical space, all has now moved to a bigger place. Lunch at Nancy's is always real good, with Helen and Dot! We pleasured the food.

Nine days on the road, nothing is better than coming home feeling ever so much prouder. Thanksgiving just passed such a memorable week, a marvelous job with great technique. Re-roofing the porch by those we hold dear, our gratitude told for many a year.

Douglas, Lori, Rick, Em, Amy and Camille were only a few who dined at our meal. Beverly, John, Max, Sean and Sophie, plus Stephen, Toni, Steve, George and Lindsay. Bud, Kim, Ruthann, John and Hannah all enjoyed our paradise right here in Georgia. Thanksgiving season and all 2009 swells our hearts the endearments of time.

God bless and keep you well.
Christmas 2009

MERRY CHRISTMAS AND HAPPY NEW YEAR

Japanese Pancakes
1 Egg• ¼ cup of All Purpose Flour • ¼ cup of Milk • 1 Tbs Butter

These ingredients are per person.
Use a separate 9" pie pan for each person.

Melt butter in pan. Mix egg, milk and flour
Pour into pan, cook at 425 for 20 min.
Eat right from the pan with syrup. This pancake forms a bowl shape.
I fill my pancake with a fried egg and link sausage.
You could use Cherries and whipped cream ~ Use your imagination!

Krazy Krackers
2 ¼ c. Unbleached flour • 2 t. Sugar • 1/2 t. Salt • ½ t. Baking Soda
½ c. Real Mayonnaise • 1 c. Plain Yogurt

In a large mixing bowl thoroughly stir together the flour, sugar, salt &
baking soda with a pastry blender. Cut in mayonnaise till well mixed &
course crumbs form.

Stir in yogurt with your hands, firmly press dough into a ball. Cut into
16 equal pieces. (First cut the ball of dough into quarters, then cut each
quarter into 1/4s.) On a prepared pastry cloth & a stockinette-covered
rolling pin, roll each piece into rounds (They will be uneven—Krazy).
Place 2 circles at a time on at a time on an ungreased sheet.
Prick with fork & sprinkle with salt.

Bake at 325 till golden (6-7 mins.)
Cool and store in tight tin.

>>>>>>>>>>>>>>>>>> **Motherhood** <<<<<<<<<<<<<<<<<<

A woman named Emily, renewing her driver's license at the
County Clerk's office, was asked by the woman recorder to state her
occupation. She hesitated, uncertain how to classify herself. "What I
mean is…" explained the recorder, "do you have a job, or are you just
a…?"

"Of course, I have a job," snapped Emily. "I'm a mother."

"We don't list 'mother' as an occupation…'housewife' covers it,'
said the recorder emphatically.

I forgot all about her story until one day I found myself in the
same situation, this time at our Town Hall. The clerk, obviously a
career woman, poised, efficient and possessed of a high sounding
title like "Official Interrogator" or "Town Registrar." "What is your
occupation?" she probed.

"What made me say it, I do not know, the words simply popped
out." "I'm a Research Associate in the field of Child Development and
Human Relations."

The clerk paused, ball-point pen frozen in mid-air, and looked up as
though she had not heard right.

I repeated the title slowly, emphasizing the most significant words.
Then I stared with wonder as my pronouncement was written in bold,
black ink on the Official questionnaire.

"Might I ask," said the clerk with new interest, "just what do you do
in your field?"

"Coolly, without any trace of fluster in my voice, I heard myself
reply, "I have a continuing program of research, in the laboratory and
in the field. "I'm working for my masters and already have four credits

(all daughters). Of course, the job is one of the most demanding in the humanities (Any mother care to disagree?), and I often work 14 hours a day. But the job is more challenging than most run-of-the-mill careers and the rewards are more of a satisfaction rather than just money."

There was an increasing note of respect in the clerk's voice as she completed the form, stood up and personally ushered me to the door.

"As I drove into our driveway, buoyed up by my glamorous new career, I was greeted by my lab assistants -age 13, 7 and 3. Upstairs I could hear our new experimental model, (6-month-old baby), in the child-development program, testing out a new vocal pattern. I felt triumphant! I had scored a beat on bureaucracy! And I had gone on the official records as someone more distinguished and indispensable to mankind than "just another mother."

Motherhood ~What a glorious career! Especially when there's a title on the door!

Does this make grandmothers "Senior Research Associates in the field of Child Development and Human Relations" and great grandmothers "Executive Senior Research Associates"? I think so!!! I think it makes Aunts "Associate Research Assistants."

Please send this to another Mother, Grandmother, Aunt and other friends you know! They will be delighted with their "new" position in life! Be loving to those who love you,

Be loving to those who do not love you and they may change.

ABOVE ALL BE YOURSELF!

Author Unknown

######### **What is a Boy?** ##########

Between the innocence of babyhood and the dignity of manhood we find a delightful creature called a boy. Boys come in assorted sizes, weights, and colors, but all boys have the same creed: To enjoy every second of every minute, of every day and to protest with noise (their only weapon) when their last minute is finished, and the adult males pack them off to bed at night.

Boys are found everywhere ~ on top of, underneath, inside of, climbing on, swinging from, running around, or jumping. Mothers love them, little girls hate them, older sisters and brothers tolerate them, adults ignore them. And Heaven protects them. A boy is Truth with dirt on its face. Beauty with a cut on its finger, Wisdom with bubble gum in its hair, and the Hope of the future with a frog in its pocket.

A boy is a composite ~~ he has the appetite of a horse, the digestion of a sword swallower, the energy of a packet-sized atomic bomb, the curiosity of a cat, the lungs of a dictator, the imagination of a Paul Bunyan, the shyness of a violet, the audacity of a steel trap, the enthusiasm of a firecracker, and when he makes something, he has five thumbs on each hand.

A boy is a magical creature ~~ you can lock him out of your workshop, but you can't lock him out of your heart. You get him put out of your study, but you can't get him out of your mind. Might as well give up ~~ he is your captor, your jailer, your boss, and your master ~~ a freckled face, pint-sized, cat-chasing, bundle of noise. But when you come home at night with only the shattered pieces of your hopes and dreams, he can mend them like new with the two magic words ~~ "Hi Dad!"

Author Unknown

Above, from Left:

Father Thomas Vigliotta, OFM, Bill Laubert, Lori Glinski, Camille Davenport, Barbara and Andrew J. Laubert, Sr., Sophia Fineran, Beverly Fineran, Ruthann Donaldson & Douglas Laubert. Witnessing 60 years of marriage!

Celebration of this happy event was held at the Foundry in Athens, Georgia on February 14th, 2012.

Our 60th wedding anniversary celebration in 2012 where 41 out of 71 relatives attended. We were originally from NJ. Our party was held in the Foundry in Athens, GA. Close to 100 guests shared our day to remember!

Andy and Barbara are showing you the two houses that Andy built. They are the two houses nearest to them. He completely rebuilt the other two. All are fine examples of his fine craftsmanship. The large shoe in the center represents "The Old Lady Who Had So Many Children She Didn't Know What To Do." It was a very good cake, enough to feed everyone.

=================**Letting Go**=================

Being connected to those you hold dear,
It's tough to "Let Go" ~ as we go through every year.
"Letting Go" is a journey, through ups and downs,
The hard times and fun times, finding rebounds.

Our parents ~ our kids, each having a place,
In our hearts filled with love, a pleasing embrace.
It starts when you're born, brought forth from the womb,
And isn't complete until we pass to the tomb.

As a child you grow ~ walking ~ talking ~ and such,
School ~ jobs ~ and marriage, all mean so much.
Leaving the nest on a journey so new,
With a partner you choose out of the blue.

Building a family is a lifelong dream,
My Prince Charming has helped with our scheme.
More than 50 years now under the bridge,
We look back in wonder ~ having 9 kids.

"Letting Go" is not easy ~ until each child finds their way,
With a new person ~ a job ~ a new place to stay.
We watch as each goes through their trials of life,
Holding our tongues, understanding their strife.

Getting older and wiser, it's our turn to care,
For our parents we knew ~ always were there.
Their time has come, we need to "Let Go,"
This surely yields ~ a tremendous blow.

Our kids are adults now, with kids of their own,
And we are the old folks ~ so much alone.
We witness the changes that living life brings,
Then marvel at all the new gadgets and things.

Most kids don't realize ~ how alone we can feel,
They're working hard ~ to provide the next meal.
So we need to step back and take a good look,
At our past and know all the hours it took.

"Letting Go" is a lesson that takes a strong heart,
Each one of our kids ~ an important part.
Wishing a lifetime of joy and content,
From your mom and dad ~ love is surely sent.

Wonderful Memories

I was a bit of an independent lady. Every now and then I needed
a vacation. My husband was not a traveler, so I would take the kids
and we'd go adventuring. I'd take them on short trips and sometimes,
longer ones. We went to Valley Forge, to Corning, where the Corning
dishes are made. On the way home we went through a cave, where
we had to go down many steps to enter the cave. We got into a boat
and took a scenic ride through the cave. Water was dripping on us,
from the ceiling of the cave, so that caused excitement and a good day.
Another time we went to Hershey to see how chocolate candy is made
and the famous Hershey Amusement Park, all these little trips were in
Pennsylvania.

One time, I drove the kids to my girlfriend's house in Llanerch, PA.
Joan Endres, she had 9 children too. I told Andy I would be staying for
a couple of days. Instead, from Joan's I drove out to my sister Mary's
in Washington, PA. I called Andy to let him know where I was, and he
said, "I figured you would do that." I stayed three days, had a great visit
with Mary and returned home feeling satisfied for a while.

On one of our usual trips to see Grandma and Nana, we stopped in
the downtown Philadelphia Mint, where we could watch how pennies
are made. From a large bar of copper that was flattened into a huge roll
of copper, then the shape of many pennies were pressed into the strip
of copper, every few seconds and dumped into very large canvas carts.
The next step was counting and rolling the pennies, for shipments to
banks. Really interesting! From there we visited Independence Hall,
the Betsy Ross House and the Liberty Bell. We often stopped along the
Willow-tree-lined Schuylkill River to have a picnic lunch. Our day was
completed with visits to our loved ones, who lived in the suburbs of
Philadelphia, often getting home quite late.

Other places we enjoyed were, without a doubt, the department
stores with the magnificent Christmas displays. John Wannamaker's
with the brilliant colored, dancing water fountain show up on the
second floor. You watched them while standing in the crowd on the first

floor, remembering too, that great big Eagle that stood near the entrance of the front door. Lit Brother's, with animated displays and rides for the youngsters. Gimbels also had fabulous Christmas decorations. This is where we could buy a special ornament for our Christmas tree.

Christmas of 1969, I drove a car full to downtown Philadelphia. We were in John Wannamaker's, at the information desk, about to go home, when I missed Douglas. He was 8 and he had gotten lost in the shoulder-to-shoulder crowd. I nearly panicked when a police officer brought him to the desk. Douglas said, "I couldn't find you, so I went outside to find a policeman." Can you imagine? He went outside on Market Street, in downtown Philadelphia. Hundreds of people shopping for Christmas! Now tell me, there truly is a gracious GOD. My faith gets stronger all the time.

We were given the opportunity to have a foreign exchange student in 1969. He was Siegfried Kohn from Germany, and was 18. Today, he is 63. Siggy spent almost a year with us, when we lived in the big house on Genoa Avenue. He always called us Mom and Daddy, that made us feel like he was our son. Siggy was a wrestler and Andy Jr. was a golfer. He and Andy Jr. were in the 12th grade at Oakcrest High School. That year we had 10 kids at home. Suppertime was always entertaining, a fun time of the day. I think back and wonder how I cooked all that food every day. What a houseful! They graduated at the same time, in June of 1970. He returned to Germany in August that same year.

Siggy and I would write letters back and forth over the years. In 1995, Siggy invited us to come to his home in Bremerhaven, on the North Sea of Germany. In his green Volkswagen car, he gave us a three-week tour of West Germany/ Fabulous! We saw many remarkable castles and everywhere we went the country was spotless, very clean and the food was delicious. Every afternoon, Siggy parked the car in some quaint little town. Usually around 3 o'clock, to have coffee and cake. Time to rest. Our drive took us to a knife and Gun Museum and an old foundry where they made big, round copper kettles, with hammers that were run by a water mill. This was fascinating.

In 1998 we visited Siggy again, to tour East Germany and
then again in 2004, to visit Bavaria. We came to a town called
Oberammergau. In this town were the most amazing carvers. You could
step into a shop and watch the artist carve. The carver was working
on a very large Eagle, he was astounding! In the same town was an
outdoor theater, where only once every ten years, actors give the
performance of the "Passion Play," during the Easter Season. We had
the privilege to take the tour of the backstage area, where the beautiful,
stunning costumes are stored, room after room. We were so fortunate!
We also had a neat experience in Oberammergau. We walked inside of
a working, running cuckoo clock. Inside we could watch the gears turn
all the clock works, to keep time. And outside in the yard of this house-
size clock, there was a little door that opened on the hour, at the peak of
the house. The birdie would come out and make its famous "Cuckoo"
sound. Siggy treated us to nearly everything, he wouldn't let us pay. He
said, "You let me live with you for free, for my education. This is what
I can do for you." What a generous man! How lucky we were.

We could never have afforded these trips, but our daughter Ruthann
was an airline attendant with Continental Airlines. Her benefits
provided passes for us to fly anywhere, for just a few dollars. This was
quite a privilege and so much appreciated. We have had many trips that
we never would have had, were it not for Ruthann's job.

In spring of 1978, I took most of the kids to upstate New York, to
see the magnificent Niagara Falls. We went because Lori's boyfriend,
Glen Steeb, was in the band from Oakcrest high School and they were
competing in a parade. It was a wonderful parade! What a joy it was to
see the Niagara River's rushing, thundering falls. A real thrill! This was
a once-in-a-lifetime event.

My high school girlfriend Joanie lives outside of Rochester, New
York. Only 90 miles from Niagara Falls, we stayed overnight at her
lovely home in Spencerport. A quaint little town situated on the Erie
Canal, just a couple of blocks from Joanie's home. That evening we all
went down to the canal to watch the houseboats and ducks float past.
Peaceful and relaxing, after a ten-hour drive north.

We have special memories of Glenn playing the piano at our house. My hubby loved to hear the song called "MacArthur Park," Glen would play it just for Andy and we all would sing. I think that Lori's senior year in high school was the best and most fun the family every had, after boyfriends came into the picture with our girls.

When Andy retired in 1992 our children had a surprise party for him. I mean it was spectacular! Beverly and John had a country home with a great big barn in the back and lots of property. The kids all pitched in to create a wonderful "Hoe Down." Douglas built a ranch-type entrance at the beginning of the long driveway. On the top of the cross bar it said, "O'TAY CORRAL." Then he made the frames for scarecrows. The girls painted and traditionally dressed them and lined both sides of the driveway. I can't remember how many scarecrows were there, but at least a dozen. A clean-up crew was needed. The old barn had to be worked on first. A huge job all by itself. Once it was cleaned out, it was set up with chairs and bales of straw for seats and the long flatbed trailer was decorated and used for a bountiful buffet, filled with all kinds of food. Speeches were made and tales were told.

Each guest was given a straw farmer's hat when they arrived. With the great big barn doors flung wide open, music played and a video of our past played continuously in the barn. I bet there were about 70 people who joined in our celebration. After dark the guys made a huge bonfire. The chairs all lined up around it and the air began getting chilly, so the fire felt good. People brought old pieces of furniture to burn. It was a roaring good time when an old chair, a couch or a table went up in flames. Boy, the young-at-heart can sure have a good time. Yes, the fire department was aware of the party and the fire. Permission was granted! Some of the younger folks hung around until early morning, keeping an eye on the fire, just to be on the safe side. This was a party to be put in the record books!

I have one more story to tell you about my "wonderful memories." Last June 23, 2013, it was my 80th birthday. Lori gave me a special party. She made President's Chicken, a meal I really enjoy, and she knows how to cook it. It was topped off with Coconut Cake and Lori's delightful Cherry Cheesecake for dessert. Dinner was over and everybody was summoned outside. The suspense increased—excitement was reverberating all around our yard. I heard a loud sound that I couldn't figure out. Then, all of a sudden, coming down the driveway was a cute white convertible. I couldn't speak—I was in disbelief! I knew that Douglas bought me a Rambler American convertible up north a year ago, but I couldn't understand how he got it shipped down here, to Georgia. I was utterly shocked! He didn't have it shipped—he bought me a different car. It was beautiful! The kids were screaming, I was crying, everyone was full of excitement! Douglas was driving my new 1963 car and going like mad around the big field, on the side of the house. THERE WERE NO BRAKES!! What a demonstration of what my car could do. I loved it!

This is how it came to be mine. Douglas moved to Georgia almost two years ago. One day he was getting gas, when a "rat rod" pulled into the gas station. Doug had a 1929 Model A Ford truck and was curious about the rat rod. He went over to the man who was driving it and they chatted for a few minutes about cars. A few weeks later we saw the man again, in a parking lot of a restaurant. Doug wanted to introduce me to him. He did, and even I, enjoyed learning a little bit about the rat rod vehicles. As time went by Doug made friends with Hudson and was going to his farm, to see the different types of vehicles that he and his friend were working on. Well, the friend of Hudson's was a man who worked in the post office, in Lexington, the same time I was the cleaning lady there. That was Grady Poole. I worked there for two years, along with Grady. That was 17 years ago! Anyway, Doug, Grady and Hudson were talking one day and Doug mentioned that he bought me the Rambler up north. It's still up there. Grady pipes up and tells Doug all about the 1963 convertible, that he was restoring for his daughter. He didn't get it done, and it's just sitting in one of Hudson's barns. Grady sold it to Doug. Lo and behold, I received this car from Doug for on June 23rd, my 80th birthday. Happiness just radiated from me! Today, it is on the road and raring to go.

As of 2014

********** *Thank You Dear Lord* **********

Thank You Dear Lord for all that You do,
I feel Your vibes when, You're not in view.
The peace that You give to soften the blows,
Is greater and pleasant than anyone knows.

To my Lord who protects and always forgives.
I awake each day with thanks I do give,
I long to be with You in Heaven one day,
Being strong in my faith, I continually pray.

My life has been full, I am content,
A great marriage, nine children,
Oh how the time went.
22 Grands, 29 G-Grands and 4 Great Great Grands.
God's blessings would fill the grandstands.

My hubby and I work side by side,
In all that we do, here at home or far and wide.
Helping our kids when their needs arise,
And enjoying the grands for the rest of our lives.

\\\\\\\\\\\\\\\\\\\\\\\\\\ **Memories of Life** ////////////////////////

I'm excited about the memories that flood back into mind.
Fulfilling me with joy so great and then that very sad kind.
My mood can swing, both high and low,
With laughter, song or tears that flow.

Times when I was oh so proud of things I did or said.
By writing stories, long and short, I hope that they'll be read.
How does one remember, incidents of so long ago?
And tell about the fun times, your readers want to know.

God helps me find the words, to write down on the paper.
He guides my pen thus I spend many hours of labor.
Recording thoughts that are etched within my mind,
Some horrible memories, then happy adventures I find.

I treasure the good times that overshadow the rest,
And trust in GOD, for He knows what's best.
Never doubting His word, I'll believe to the end,
That Jesus my Lord is truly my friend.

February 15, 2015

>>>>> **Merry Christmas 2015** <<<<<

Oh, by gee by golly, I need to find some holly.
Only 3 more days until Christmas.
I'm late writing cards and wrapping gifts.
I have many thanks to send, a curtain to mend,
Plus, many odd jobs to make everything nice,
Like a pumpkin pie, with just the right spice.

We'll stretch out our table and add more, if need be,
To share in a meal—of veggies, ham, and turkey.
The good Lord takes care of us day after day,
Believing and trusting, He'll show us the way.
Think positive—embrace—all the good things,
All around us are examples, of LOVE that He brings.

Let me reflect on the year that is spent,
Days, weeks, and months—oh how they went,
I'm slow doing chores, whenever I do,
Strength and energy are down to a few,
Making a trip is a lot of fun,
but EXHAUSTION SETS IN WHEN IT'S ALL DONE.

* * * * * * * * * * * * * * * * *

*Mid July Andy drove us to Brunswick for the wedding of
Melissa Kowalchuk. And a visit with my dear friend Joyce. We
were there for only one day, which made our visit quite short. The
wedding was beautiful, but Hot—melting hot! Phewie! Doreen
(Melissa's mom & Joyce's daughter) made us extra comfy for a
night's stay, then back home the next day.*

May the happiness you feel today,
Continue through the years,
The memories you will cherish,
Sometimes they're mixed with tears.
Keeping our Lord within your heart,
Your marriage will grow strong,
Warding off temptation, guarding you from wrong.
Be true with love and patience until you're old and gray,
Remembering how you started out,
Way back to TODAY.
July 11, 2015

Many Thanks

In August Andy drove us to visit with Bud and Kim in Gulfport, Mississippi. We stayed 3 Days, making this a 5-day trip. Bud always shows us a terrific time. We usually eat out, cause Bud doesn't cook or like the mess. We have fun at the casinos even though we don't win and sometimes we just drive around to see the sights. Bud's a great tour guide and always has a new car, so we get a chance to have rides in a different car each year. Now back at Bud's (my brother) where it's quiet, there's a better opportunity to have easier conversation than on the phone, since we're both hard of hearing.

He's 4 years older than I am at 82.

A couple years ago Bud decided I needed a 'Salt & Pepper' collection; within two years he gave me at least 130 pairs. Andy had to build shelves to show them off. I have Salt & Pepper shakers for every occasion, season, or birthday.

Thank you, my dear brother it's so comforting to know, that I still have family.

>>>>>>> **Tender Loving Memories** <<<<<<<

Tender loving memories, a gift within my heart,
To reminisce and feel the joy, all started with a car.
My 51 convertible, the color was powder blue,
He asked me for a ride you see—so what else was I do?

I only knew him from our school, where he was the football star,
He wore dungarees and a white tee shirt I had noticed from afar.
I drove him to the river where we laughed and shared our lives,
A penny for your thoughts I'd say and wonder his replies.

I know I fell in love that day; my heart was all a jitter,
Then he asked me for a real date; that made my eyelids twitter.
We only had those two dates because the Navy was his call,
Where his duties on the 123 were in the damage control.

Playing baseball while on the ship was a joy he'll long remember.
The Med cruise and on to Rio were just a few ports of splendor.
Writing letters every day, because the love bug bit,
We grew to know each other; our friendship was a hit.

Just six weeks out to sea when my man was missing me,
He wrote about a penny for his thoughts that filled me with glee.
He asked me in a letter—would you be my wife,
I wrote right back and said; "Yes, I'll give you my life."

He took a mail plane back to the states; it took 5 long days,
Surprising me at my job and seeing him took my breath away.
His new orders were for fire fighting school in Philly,
Weekend dates were better than writing letters that were silly.

Three months went by—our wedding plans were set,
February 16th, 1952—only 6 months from when we met.
Now it's been 65 years and we're still in love,
With our God's protection, he is my turtle-dove

October 9, 2016

>>>>>> **Lori** <<<<<<

What a special birthday! You went over the top with
making soooo many people happy!

I was extra surprised with my cake.
You did a splendid job!
You put so much on your plate to please your
Glinski family and even found the inspiration to build
my favorite hobby into a cake. Thank you for making me feel
special; along with having all of your hubby's family to also
help me celebrate; eating that sumptuous cake—-It was delicious!

I hope by now, your back is rested and your feet don't hurt.
Please know that I had a wonderful birthday and have shared
my excitement with many of my friends and your siblings.
I love you very much,

Mom
June 30, 2018

Our son Billy

This is our son Billy *(see right hand page)*.

He experienced many troubles during his teenage years. He squared
himself away by the time he married Barbara Chiappini. Married
now for 22 years. We are so proud of Billy today because he's a
perfectionist with any work on his huge house or 63' sailboat.
His craftsmanship is remarkable!

>>>>>>>>>> **Billy** <<<<<<<<<<<

Oh, Billy, we love you.
Where else can I start?
It's just plain awful,
To be far apart!

We want you to know,
That you're welcome at home,
When you make up your mind,
To leave the devil alone.

He's corrupted your mind,
Your body and soul,
And it's left in our hearts,
A mighty big hole.

This poem was written during the 70's—those teenage years.

My Dear Joyce

You sent me the sunshine to brighten my day,
I'm sending it back to help YOU find a way.
To ease the turmoil down deep inside,
The Good Lord is with you; He'll be your guide.

Trust Him and love Him, with all of your heart,
In His time you'll see, how He does His part.
Repairing the hurts, I'm sure that's His plan,
Making your LIFE, feel whole once again,

Love you sincerely,
my dear friend,

Barbara

December 7, 2015

\\\\\\\\\\\\\\\\\\\\\\\ **Dear LORD** ///////////////////

Dear Lord, dear LORD, please show me the way,
To understand the changes of living today.

The world is in turmoil; it's turned upside down,
It confuses the mind; I continually frown.

Words that are spoken, or ideas my kids share,
Tear me apart—never being aware.

Reacting to this handed down misinformation,
It causes for tears and confounded questions.

I can't believe, after trying so hard, I am rejected,
My world is so different from what I expected.

I always wanted a big family to love and to share,
Having laughs at the table, knowing everyone cared.

Here I am at 83, if only I knew how to handle the lies,
Dear LORD, my heavy heart looks up toward the skies.

Oh, help me I cry, please smooth the way,
Let me feel it tomorrow to start a new day.

I trust in you LORD, yes You have the plan,
Now let me live it the best that I can.

After my broken arm
May 11, 2016

********** **Dear Carol** **********

"Thank You," is such an inadequate phrase,
Just can't find the words to cover those days.
That you cared, shared, and helped me through,
Being sincere because the love shines in you.

Please accept the gratitude I try to express,
Sometime ~ somehow ~ God surely will bless,
Your family and friends, Carol and Glen,
I don't know how; I don't know when.

Love, Barbara

Happy Birthday Bud
~~~ Oh My Gosh, 88!

As I look around my house and see,
All the things you've given to me.

My heart sings remembering you,
Wishing to visit for a day or two.

But life turns we don't expect,
Slowing us down makes time to reflect.

On the good times that well overflow,
With happiness and joy your gifts bestow.

So much fun at casinos and places to eat,
Emptied our pockets, then finding a treat.

Dear Bud, we love you and miss you,
We wish we lived near,
Have a happy birthday with those you hold dear.

Our love, Andy & Barbara
July 19, 2017

Hi, Dear Billy

****

Hi dear Billy, you make my day,
It brings me joy in a special way.
I can see your smile with a pleasant hello,
And a laugh that gives me, a warm shining glow.

Memories we've shared about times gone past,
Your ambitions right now, I'm sure will last.
You're a man, of whom I'm oh so proud,
That you are my son; I'd shout it out loud.
The journey's been tough and has turned out right,
Your Barbara's your strength, so hold her tight.
Your tomorrows may be many, we really don't know,
But working together has created a great show.

Your home an example of your efforts side by side,
And the boat is another work; you can't even hide.
Both, of these labors have proven to be,
Show pieces of work done diligently.

I pray for good health, for Barbara and you,
Sharing joys and love with your family too.
Many years of marriage—your destiny- who knows?
Trips to Long Island, to see Danielle and the boys.
Hillary too, is a big part of your life,
Until she grew up and became Skip's wife.
All, of these things are treasures to keep,
Enjoying the everyday, no reason to weep.

My Billy, have fun in whatever you do,
Till you're old and tired and the jobs become few.
We all come to see life, in different ways,
Shape yours to be hearts in those later days.
I love you my son, you've proven to me,
That God answers prayers, this I can see.
Keep well and live on to accomplish your dreams,
Fulfill all your hopes with wonderful schemes.

Love, Mom

############### **As I Awake Today** ****###############

As I awake today with the joys of yesteryear,
rolling round my head,
I find a burst of happenings that keep me here in bed.

Dear brother Bud, Hazel and of course George and Kim.
Fill me with happiness, salt and peppers, good times surrounding them.

Visits back and forth to Mississippi or Georgia it could be,
Welcoming each other and making memories so joyfully.

Dinner in Casinos or a walk-through Shaking Rock
A brother sister friendship grew tight as if a solid block.

Many rides on US 90, seeing sites of growth, others of despair,
The rebound of hope and life as humans work to repair.

The beauty of the sea brings the waves of tranquility,
A soothing calm to rest the mind with dreams of entity.

Turkey and Ham have been a favorite meal to share,
With brother Bud and all of us, as we laugh enjoying fare.

The love that's grown between us ~ siblings such as we,
Is hard to explain ~ it's deep and strong and high as you can see.

So glad we moved to Georgia, for a treasure I would have missed,
Is a joy that keeps on coming as the years turn into bliss.

Thank you, dear Bud, I cherish all you've done,
For me ~ your sister, who loves you ~ one on one.

P.S. The word 'entity' means: real existence or existence in the mind

January 1, 2017

(((((((((жжжжж **Dr. Larry Medders** жжжжж)))))))))

What a doctor—what a man,
He's the best, I'm his greatest fan.

His skill is unique, a specialist very rare,
Soft manner of voice expressing his care.

He works with the bones that structure our frame,
Mending the breaks, torn biceps and those I can't name.

He gives you the confidence to make it through,
The many weeks of healing,'til you're like new.

Three operations this fine doctor performed,
On an old lady, who somehow gets torn?

From her fingers to her shoulder, are just like before,
I'm grateful and I thank you, I hope there is no more.

I'd like to mention your interests, outside of your career,
Are building and gardening where you'll see new things appear.

Maybe a desk for a grandchild you'll build,
Or the flowers you planted will give you a thrill?

Who knows what's really in store,
You're healthy and happy, NOW live on for more.

July 12, 2017

Merry Christmas 2018

What a whirlwind this year has been! From doctors and hospitals and home safe and sound. Now all is well. Best of all is that we still love it here at "Paradise Found." The weather's not freezing, there is no ice storm yet and the electric hasn't gone off. Wow! What more could we want?

Andy and I do not travel much anymore. It takes a lot f energy and we have slowed down. I'm 85 and Andy is 88. He recently finished a very big job building 48 seven-foot shutters for an 1800-something antebellum house. Yes, the house had 24 windows that used the job. The stress was too much for him, as he wound up in the hospital about a week after completing the work. No more big jobs! BUT he still does little repairs on antique furniture and more.

We did make a trip to visit our families. Beverly and John make us feel welcome in their home. Max is engaged to Sutton, and Sean has finished college as a cartoon artist. Sophie is a joy and an honor student. She just turned 13 this month.

We got to visit Pam and Dave Crawford (our niece and we adopted Dave as our loving son—Ha) laughing aside, we do love him as a son. He makes us proud. He has a fabulous talent carving with chainsaws. We also visited my friend Nancy Herbert, who invited us to lunch. She served homemade clam chowder. Nancy's been my friend since we were 15 years old. I got to be with Joyce Breder, another dear friend since 1953 who lives in Bordentown, NJ. All these visits brought about new memories shared with old friends. Such a delight!

Doug had a shoulder operation, cataract surgery, in the hospital again for dehydration and then learned his kidneys only had 50% function! Need I say more?

I had surgery on both hands due to Carpal Tunnel and Trigger Fingers. I'm healing very well. We appreciate all the prayers, food, phone calls and love you've extended to us during our many hospital experi-

*This was Christmas dinner when I served 31—all relatives (1992).
I prepared the meal alone and I just loved it!*

*Andy built this room to look like you were eating in a fancy restaurant.
It has beautiful colonial blue beams with white wood tiles in between
the beams.*

And so much more!

ences during 2018. We've recovered and with your help we made it.

Just one more serious concern is that just this week, Doug had a mini-stroke. He is at high risk for a full-blown stroke due to high blood pressure, cholesterol, and diabetes. Please keep him in your prayers once more, and thanks in advance.

Our son Greg came to visit us twice a year and believe me it's good to see him. He makes us feel so special to him. It's a 12-hour drive from NJ to our house. Bringing tidings of great joy, but his visits are usually only about 12 hours.

We're all in good spirits—after all, "The Lord is with us always." So, as my Grandmother Wilson always said, "Look for the Good," and I try to do just that.

Have a healthy New Year.

Our love and good wishes to our dear friends and family, Barbara & Andy,

Mom & Dad

Chapter 5

During the Winter of My Life

*** A Turning Point in Life ***

Eighty some years ~ they came and went,
Some with applause and some tears were spent.
We've reached a turning point ~ making changes,
Life's needs are now ~ in different ranges.

Our blessings abound ~ a valued treasure,
Heartfelt feelings have unlimited measure.
With the Lord as our Savior, there's always a way,
He brings us peace, at the end of each day.

Christmas this year, will be different you see,
As these two old folks forge on courageously.
Our time has come, to sit back watching the joys,
While our young families can buy all the toys.

I guess what I'm really trying to say.
Now it's your turn to do things your way.
Our family now numbers a big sixty-nine,
Oh, what a splendid family line.

***************** **Christmas Dinner** *****************

I'm writing this note to invite you to our home for "The BAG"
and treats at: 7:00 o'clock. This will be on December 25, 2019, a
Wednesday ~ Jesus' Birthday.

I know you're all very tired after a busy day,
But come share "The Bag" in Gram's special way.

God has given us a few extra years,
Hoping we all get together, for fun and good cheers.

So, I saved up more stuff, to put in "The Bag."
A tradition that carries a very low ~ price tag.

I've searched and gathered for lots of fun things,
Hoping your pick is just right when ~ out of the bag your dig brings.

Only the laughter and joy as we reach in to find,
Something we need or that throw away kind.

The comments ring loud, as we dig deep once more,
Hoping to feel the very best gift is a chore.

So please come and join us to share the love,
That God has allowed us, from way up above.

These two old folks need just a bit of your time,
We know time is precious ~ just come and unwind.

With our love,
Gram & Pop

~+~+~+~+~+~+~+ **Christmas 2019** +~+~+~+~+~+~+~+

Twas just 8 days before Christmas ~ when all thru the house,
Came the buzz baking cookies and no time for a mouse.

Finished our shopping and wrapping has become such a chore,
I've grown 'old' during this year ~ my back is so sore.

Not to complain ~ I've come to realize that time takes its toll,
We're a whole lot slower or taking a fall ~ we can't even roll.

The gifts are all mailed ~ how meager they be,
But all filled with much love, for our blessed family.

You've ALL shared in a dream that we could for-see,
We did our best, with no books to help me.

Now my dear friends I want to convey,
How you've given us very memorable days.

The visits, communion, at times out to lunch,
Enjoy your company, a great big whole bunch.

Merry Christmas and Happy New Year ~ to one and all,
We're wishing good health and happiness,
We hope that you ~ have a BALL!

Our love,
Barbara & Andy

****** Here's How ******

How do we say all the things that we feel?
How do we show our intentions are real?

How do we share all the love that's inside?
When life is on such a turbulent ride!

We overcame money, disappointment, and strife,
Pursuing significant directions in life.

Living to be both moral and fair,
Sometimes we find ~ only despair.

Our hearts grow so heavy, when life throws us a curve,
And our minds wander off ~ to swing and to swerve.

The secret is JESUS ~ He'll show us the way,
If we let HIM in ~ He's there to stay.

A positive attitude we must reveal,
For those around us ~ to learn how to deal.

Unconditional love spills over the brim,
Into our hearts, through GOD, please know HIM.

****** **Our Love for Evelyene** *******
Happy 80th Birthday

Twenty-five years have flown right by,
Since God brought us to Georgia, I now know why.
To meet a dear friend, who was 55 back then.
She watched her grandkids, until who knew when.

Our friendship grew, with visits at her house or mine,
Just two curving miles to John Moon's sign.
Her great hubby gave us a ride, in the back of his truck,
Riding the back roads and creeks, I feared we'd get stuck.

I needed to visit my kids who were still living up north,
To New Jersey was 1500 miles of roads back and forth.
My new-found friend came along for the ride,
We stayed at Nancy's, in a room she happily did provide.

Over the years Evelyene, we have shared our talents,
We appreciate each other's accomplishments.
You shared your veggies, and I hemmed your slacks,
We couldn't keep up with each other's tracks.

And Wow! Turning 80 is a good long life,
With Bud by your side, 'cause you are his wife.
Now Evelyene, you are the best friend all of us know.
So rest, take it easy, enjoying a bright new tomorrow.

Our love, Barbara and Andy

Since That First Ride

It's been a good ride since that little blue car,
Started us off for a journey thus far.
A few weeks back I turned eighty-eight,
We've spent 70 years since our first date.,
God granted our wishes and dreams come true.
Our children—there's nine—with no book on "How To."

Daddy built a back yard with gym bars, slides, and swings,
I made lots of clothes, toys, curtains and many more things.
Together we've supported each one, in their hour of need,
Now there's help from above, wishing you all God's speed.

Hard work and struggles, that's part of God's plan.
To build a strong marriage—the best that we can,
All nine adults, are now out on their own,
Endeavoring to establish integrity shown.

Remember! Prayers ARE answered I have a list of a few,
My blind eye seeing again, and life wasn't over, who knew?
I am so grateful to live on the tears easily flow,
Crying for joy—oops now a nose to blow.

A mother's love is so deep deep—deep.
Each one in my heart to keep keep—keep.
Warm hugs and love are sent your way,
Sincere happy wishes, for you day after day.

Oh—so Sincerely,
Mama

May 9, 2013 revised 2021

>>>>>>>>>> Happy Birthday Bud<<<<<<<<<<

Oh Bud, how wonderful it's been to share,
The many visits of interest and such tasty fare.
You're a darn good host, so generous and kind,
You drive us around to new sites that you find.

We enjoy your daughter, she's a lot of fun,
Playing "Sequence" is a challenge to be won.
Snacks and a drink are a treat we enjoy,
At George and Kim's house we played, oh boy.

The casinos are exciting ~ maybe we'll win,
Pennies or quarters ~ just watch the wheels spin.
Three or four pictures line up in a row,
Making us happy with smiles that glow.

The salt and peppers you've given to me,
Bring conversations that fill us with glee.
Thanksgiving with pumpkins and figures that pray,
Add to the festivities, for a very special day.

The clock in our bathroom keeping good time,
Tablecloth and napkins are favorites of mine.
So many things, I've mentioned only a few,
Pleasures we enjoy, because of you.

Being together means oh so much,
A card or a call ~ just keeping in touch.
Who would believe we could make it this far?
To delight in the friendship as siblings we are.

Thank you, my brother, for being so true,
To a sister who ~ sincerely loves you.
Happy Birthday with love from Andy and me,
Have ice cream and cake, our Ce ~ leb ~ rity!

Our love,
Barbara and Andy

Who Ever Knew?

    Dear Bud, A wonderful brother who loves us.
He said, 'Come on down,' so we went on a bus.
Sharing your family, welcoming us there,
In Gulfport, Miss. We enjoyed specialty fare.

    There is no other who has been true to me,
Entertaining, encouraging and so lovingly,
How very important it is to share real time,
Sometimes at your place, others at mine.

    Marvelous shows and meals, all were so good.
A wonderful host who really knows food.
Your lovely home, the best you did offer,
Must have put a dent in your coffer.

    Please realize dear Bud, you're one of a kind,
You're generous, admirable, a match hard to find.
We love you my brother, from way back when,
A void 30 years and now enjoying eight plus two times ten.

    "Who Ever Knew" we'd be such friends?
Yes, siblings who found each other again.
Have a wonderful Birthday, wish we could be there,
To shower you with love that all of us share.

    Ninety ~ two years has been quite a road traveled,
And "Who Ever Knew" has all of us baffled,
Except the dear Lord, He knows it all.
So when you need help, give HIM a call.

    I pray for you many times during the week.
I only wish you could hear me when I try to speak.
Phone calls are a challenge, so I continue to pray,
And I'll write letters, to let you know what I say.

Love, Barbara & Andy
July 19, 2022

It's been a good ride since that little blue car,
Started us off for a journey thus far.
In a few weeks I will be eighty ~ eight,
We've spent 69 years since that first date.
God granted our wishes and dreams come true,
Our children ~ there are nine ~ with no book on "How To."

Hard work and struggles, that's part of God's plan,
To build a strong marriage ~ the best that we can.
All nine adults are now out on their own,
Endeavoring to establish integrity shown.

Daddy built a back yard with gym bars, slides, and swings,
I made lots of clothes, toys, curtains and many more things.
Together we've tried to support each child, in their hour of need,
Now there's help from above ~ wishing you all God's speed.

Remember! Prayers ARE answered—I have a list of a few,
My blind eye is seeing again and my life,
near dying when who knew?
I am so grateful ~ the tears easily flow,
Crying for joy ~ oops a nose to blow.

I love you all ~ so deep ~ deep ~ deep,
Each one in my heart to keep ~ keep ~ keep.
Warm hugs and love are sent your way,
With happy wishes for this is the Day!

Oh ~so sincerely,
Mama

May 14, 2023

Never Forget Your Friends

A newly young man sitting on the porch on a humid day, sipping iced tea with his father. As he talked about adult life, marriage, responsibilities and obligations, the father thoughtfully stirred the ice cubes in his glass and cast a clear sober look on his son.

"Never forget your friends," he advised, "they will become more important as you get older." Regardless of how much you love your family and the children you happen to have; you will always need friends. Remember to go out with them occasionally (if possible) but keep in contact with them somehow.

"What strange advice!!" thought the young man. "I just entered the married world, I am an adult and surely my wife and the family that we will start, will be everything I need to make sense of my life.

Yet, he obeyed his father, kept in touch with his friends and annually increased their number. Over the years he became aware that his father knew what he was talking about, in as much as time and nature carry out their designs and mysteries on a person, friends are the bulwarks of our life ~ After 60, 70, 80 years of life, here is what he (and you) will have learned.

Time passes ~ Life goes ~ The distance separates ~ Children grow up. Children cease to be children and become independent ~ And to parents, it breaks their hearts, but the children are separated from the parents. Jobs come and go. ~ Illusions, desires, attraction, sex ~ weakens.

People do not do what they should do ~ The heart breaks, the parents die, colleagues forget the favors, the races are over. ~ But true friends are always there, no matter how long or how many miles away they are. A friend is never more distant than the reach of a need, intervening in your favor, waiting for you with open arms or in some way blessing your life.

When we started this adventure called LIFE, we did not know of the incredible joys or sorrows that were ahead. WE did not know how much we would need from each other. Love your parents, take care of your children, but keep a group of good friends. ~ Dialog with them. ~ But do not impose your criteria.

Send this to your friends (even those you seldom see) who help make sense of your life, I just did!

Author Unknown

This is a 10" tall bouquet made with crystal seed beads held in a crystal vase. I made this to commemorate our 70 years of marriage. 1952 too 2022!

The lane to our hearts,
Is warm day by day,
Because of the friends,
We meet along the way.

We can do without pressure,
That sometimes gives pain.
But not without friends,
On that cheery old lane.

By my Grandma

Grandma Wilson
My mentor lived to be 96

Grandma crocheted
this hat plus 50 more!

*******Trusting*********

There is no intervention,
There is no love or tears,
There is no understanding,
all these many years.
We've rescued, loved, and cared,
We've hoped, prayed and stared,

I give her - to You dear Lord,
With TRUST and FAITH,
I'll wait - on my own accord.

Some day we'll know,
She's found the way,
To end this dreadful wrath,
By trusting YOU and understanding,
Then choosing a new path.

I thank YOU Lord for listening,
To my plea of consolation,
Knowing that -YOU will,
Heal this heartfelt situation.

P.S. She has found peace
after 35 years. Now she can enjoy her family!
Trusting in our LORD!

\\\\\\\\\ **My Only Dear Cousin, Ann Cowart** /////////

Love and prayers I will convey,
Over the miles so far away.
We're like blood sisters, thru and thru,
Just can't stop thinking of you!
Ocean City such fun on the beach,
Our families together; sand, water and treats.

Thanksgiving dinner at your house or mine,
We shared in festivities ~ so very fine.
Hand me down clothes from your cousins so dear,
Made me so happy, I had to cheer.
Walking to school, meeting our friends,
We laughed and talked, with no money to spend.

Finding our man ~ the love of our life, our husbands to be,
we their wife.
Into adults ~ yes, we finally grew, starting a life ever so new.
Building a family with love it did bind, you had two boys and
kids ~ I had nine.
Now over the years ~ always in touch,
Coast to coast visits were never too much.

Thank you, dear Ann, for loving me,
I'll treasure the wonderful memories,
My love continues over the miles,
Hoping this poem brings back some smiles.

Love, Barb

****

January 5, 2006;
Later this day Ann passed away after hearing the poem. She came out
of a week long coma and said "tell Barbie to keep on writing."

<<<<< **A Remembrance of Ann** <<<<<
<<<<< *By her Husband Clyde Cowart* <<<<<

Ann has crossed a narrow bridge that spans a deep abyss,
And now she sits in wondrous awe before Christ's holy face.
We hear the Savior say, "Well done my faithful one.
Come, sit here in this place."

With heart so full, about to burst, she does as He commands,
And then receives the just reward from her Savior's hands.
The life she lived while here on earth was one of quiet faith,
She let her life speak out to all of Jesus' saving grace.

We miss her deeply, that is true, she blessed us all each day,
But now she serves a greater call in a far different way.
No more sufferings, no more weary days

For Christ has called her home you see
and healed her in so many ways.

God's Plan

God's beautiful plan is sometimes concealed,
But some day His purpose will be revealed.

Someday God's wisdom will make it very plain,
Why problems were permitted and how He uses pain.

Things thought logical - "Disease, tragedy, fear -
Will someday make sense when God makes all things clear.

We'll see the Lord's purpose from Heaven's point of view,
And we will understand in ways we never knew.

Till we are home with God, some answers have to wait,
"Lord, we'll TRUST AND OBEY, LORD help us walk by FAITH.

Author Unknown

A Prayer for All Souls Day

Most Sacred Heart of Jesus, in your compassion and your love, we entrust to your merciful heart the soul of our departed who have gone before us in faith. We hope in Your promise that all who seek you will find eternal life – a place of refreshment, light and peace, forever and ever. Amen.

~~~~~ **When I Pass to Eternal Life!** ~~~~~

Now I lay me down to sleep,
To dream the dreams that I will reap.

With peace of mind, through the good Lord above,
With forgiveness, He showered me with love.

I'll dance to the tunes the angels will play,
Enjoying new time with loved ones all day.

I'll see each one's face and smile with glee,
He told me I'd see them again so happily.

I'm thankful dear Lord for the comfort You bring,
To my heart and body, erasing everyday sting.

Just knowing You are right there by my side,
Has given me a much smoother ride.

I look forward to this new place,
Of contentment, joy, and Your Loving Embrace.

To say THANK YOU dear Lord, is much too short,
For Your gift of Eternal Life, that IS brought forth.

May 1, 2021

Dear Charles & Kathy,

Our Testimonial for Charles and Kathy Steelman's 50th Wedding Anniversary, January 13, 2018

Kathy, you were just a little girl, maybe nine or ten years old. When Uncle Andy met your dad while working on a job one day. Your dad was an electrician and your Uncle Andy worked in construction.

Andy was building our first new home, in Egg Harbor City, NJ in 1953. Your dad offered to do the wiring in exchange, Andy transformed your front porch into a bedroom for your sister Debbie.

Your mother became my dearest friend over the years, as our husbands continued to barter their talents, helping each family as time went by. Andy dropped the ceiling in your living room, built a beautiful kitchen and made a nice bathroom, while your dad wired the addition on our first home and then he wired our even bigger second home.

As the years went by, you, Kathy, met Charley Steelman and planned a wedding for January 13, 1968. I was in Shore Memorial Hospital at the time, but I was being discharged from the hospital that day. The reception restaurant was just down the street from the hospital, so I had a friend take me to the reception. I didn't want to miss out on seeing the "Bride and Groom."

Great friends ~ and we watched you, Carol and Debbie, grow. Jane was married and away from home. Your mother, Mary, planted the seed of knowing the LORD in my life, for which I am ever-grateful. We grew to be like family, a gift that's lasted a lifetime.

Kathy and Charles, you have continued to make us feel like your family. After moving to Georgia, you both have helped us through some tough times, for which we sure do appreciate all of your love and support. Kathy, thank you for taking me shopping for the clothes I was able to wear to our son's wedding in Ireland. I want to mention that our first daughter, Ruthann, was an airline attendant, so we could fly to Ireland for pennies.

We'll never forget the wonderful opportunity to work for Michael and Scott in Cumming, GA. Plus the many gifts over the last 25 years, that you and Charley have given us. Even the kitchen sink (that was from an old house that was torn down). And Charley's old Dell computer. I loved it and kept it running for many years.

Your loving children, Kim and John, have also been a pleasure, to see their lives blossom and be filled with the new experiences and endeavors they tackle along the way. Especially the grandchildren that you enjoy today.

50 years of marriage is quite a milestone. Let happiness and love continue through the years with understanding and tenderness. May the good LORD watch over you and care for you all the days of your lives.

Our sincere love,

Aunt Barbara & Uncle Andy

August 31, 2012

~~~ **Thank You Kim** ~~~

I woke up this morning with Kathy on my mind,
She's been so special, a dear friend of mine.
She helped me know God,
Inspiring me with, the way I should trod.

Dear Kim, Our most sincere thoughts are with you,
To show your care and love for your parents true.
Oh how we commend you for the sacrifices you've made,
Your hubby and children support you, surely that's great.

You are loyal, unselfish, overwhelmingly kind,
Very few hours to rest and unwind.
A daughter, a sister, best friend, wife and mother,
Even including when helping out with your brother.

I'll try to explain how your family has cared for us both,
Enjoying a lunch and a ride in the fun pontoon boat.
Outfitting me for my son's wedding in Ireland we went.
And help from my daughter, a flight attendant.

They shared their friends Michael and Scott,
Who asked Andy to do a big job.
Building a stairway and even more,
Paying us well to even the score.

How proud she was to show us the new project,
So many houses are spaced attractively correct.
An old house was torn down, and Kathy gave us the sink.
For our remodeled kitchen, gratefully accepted without a blink.

You are cheerful with friends and the people you meet,
A serious mind at your job can't be beat.
Directing all departments is a mountainous chore,
To be sure there are no open doors.

Money for Christmas—a very special gift.
Our jaws drop, but oh what a lift.
So many suppers or snacks on the run,
Or wonderful visits were always such fun.

Kim, what a journey you've traveled thus far,
These are the paths that have proven you a bright star,
Caring for your parents, friends and loved ones,
Kim, you're very special when all's said and done.

Please read this to Kathy,
Love & prayers,
Aunt Barbara & Uncle Andy

July 13, 2021

********** **The Bright Road Ahead** **********

My darling, you're special. Surely God knows,
What a tough road, and so many blows.
We talk of a tunnel with a light at the end,
You're on the journey and turning the bend.

The family you love and want to unite,
Is waiting on that road; don't give up the fight.
Our hearts are so lifted, seeing the change,
Back to a mom who can make dinners again.

Cleaning and painting and laughing, oh boy!
I just cannot tell you, what a wonderful joy!
The light's getting brighter, and the work has begun,
You'll make it, my dear hopes and dreams can be fun.

Think of the good times and make future, plans,
Then you'll see your efforts fill in your demands.
Our prayers will continue till you've accomplished your goal,
Let the past be gone, no longer taking its toll.

1995

EVERLASTING LOVE

SUBMITTED PHOTO

Andy and Barbara Laubert are celebrating their 70th wedding anniversary this week. They have nine children, 23 grandchildren, 32 great-grandchildren and four great-, great-grandchildren. Andy Laubert, 91, built two homes and remodeled two others for his family. He also built three houses for others in his spare time. Andy is skilled in building cabinets, masonry and fabrication. Barbara, 88, is a skilled seamstress, an artist who works with tiny seed beads, wrote a memoir and is about to publish her second book of poetry: "Over The Years I Found Peace."

Dear Mary,

My love extends beyond my reach,
And thanks for all the good things you teach.

Your knowledge comes from your
GOD up above,
You've taught me to live and share
HIS Love.

Happy Birthday, my friend, I'd like
to impart,
It comes from way down ~~~~
deep in my heart.

Love always your friend,
Barbara

To Mary Thaxton, June 6th

And Then it Is Winter…

You know…time has a way of moving quickly and catching you unaware of the passing years. It seems just yesterday that I was young, just married and embarking on my new life with my mate.

Yet in a way, it seems like eons ago and I wonder where all the years went. I know that I lived them all. I have glimpses of how it was back then and all my hopes and dreams. But, here it is…the winter of my life and it catches me by surprise... How did I get here so fast?

Where did the years go and where did my youth go?

I remember well seeing older people through the years and thinking that those older people were years away from me and that winter was so far off that I could not fathom it or imagine fully what it would be like. But, here it is…my friends are retired and getting gray…they move slower and I see an older person now. Some are in better and some worse shape than me…but, I see the great change ….Not like the ones that I remember who were young and vibrant…but, like me, their age is beginning to show and we are now those older folks that we used to see and never thought we'd be.

Each day now, I find that just getting a shower is a real target for the day! And taking a nap is not a treat anymore…it's mandatory! Cause if I don't on my own free will... I just fall asleep where I sit. And so... now I enter into this new season of my life unprepared for all the aches and pains and the loss of strength and ability to go and do things that I wish I had done but never did!

But, at least I know that through the winter has come and I'm not sure how long it will last... this I know, that when it's over on this earth…it's NOT over. A new adventure will begin!

Yes, I have regrets. There are things I wish I hadn't done...but indeed, there are many things I'm happy to have done. It's all in a lifetime.

So, if you're not in your winter yet...let me remind you, that it will be here faster than you think. So, whatever you would like to accomplish in your life please do it quickly! Don't put things off too long!

Life goes by quickly. So, do what you can today, as you can never be sure whether this is your winter or not! You have no promise that you will see all the seasons of your life... so, live for today and say all the things that you want your loved ones to remember... and hope that they appreciate and love you for all the things that you have done for them in all the years past!

"Life" is a gift to you from God." The way you live your life is your gift to those who come after you. Make your's a fantastic one.

LIVE IT WELL! ENJOY TODAY! DO SOMETHING FUN! BE HAPPY! HAVE A GREAT DAY!

REMEMBER
It is health that is real wealth and not pieces of gold and silver.

LIVE HAPPY IN THIS YEAR AND EVERY YEAR!

LASTLY, CONSIDER THE FOLLOWING; TODAY IS THE OLDEST YOU'VE EVER BEEN, YET THE YOUNGEST YOU'LL EVER BE, SO—ENJOY THIS DAY WHILE IT LASTS.

~Your kids are becoming you...

~Going out is good...Coming home is better!

~You forget names...But it's OK because other people forgot they even knew you!!!

~You realize you're never going to be really good at anything... especially golf...

~The things you used to care to do, you no longer care to do, but you really do care that you don't care to do.

~You sleep better on a lounge chair with the TV blaring than in bed. It's called "pre-sleep."

~You miss the days when everything worked with just an "ON" and "OFF" switch... You tend to use more 4 letter words.."what?.."when?".."what?"

~You notice everything they sell in stores is "sleeves"?!!!

~What used to be freckles are now liver spots.

~Everybody whispers.

~You have 3 sizes of clothes in your closet...
2 of which you will never wear again.

!But Old Songs, Old movies, and best of all, OLD FRIENDS!!

Stay well, "Old FRIEND!"

It's Not What You Gather, But What You Scatter That Tells What Kind Of Life You Have Lived.

And Then It's Winter…

<<<<<<<<<<<<<<< **Time** >>>>>>>>>>>>>>>

Good morning world… Life is a journey that takes us near and far away. It's all about TIME. Having TIME for work, sleep or play. Even a TIME to eat to give us the energy to do all of these things and also taking TIME to relax.

How we spend it and how we waste our precious TIME on this earth. When I think back, trying to remember the many times that have been important, happy or sad, it fills me with wonder or joy or even amazement to realize how much TIME has gone by.

Did you ever think about "TIME" ? It's never here nor there. You can tell TIME with a clock (we have over a hundred in Andy's collection), a watch, the Sun or a sundial and with an hourglass.

What TIME is it?

"It's Merry Christmas TIME— 2018" You can be on TIME or behind TIME. And then, you can have the TIME of your life. Situations determine how we spend our TIME. Well, I don't have the TIME to go or to stay. Some TIMES we have it, or don't have it and other TIMES we just ride it out.

TIME—often TIME goes too slow, fast or feels like it is at a standstill. You need patience to wait for somebody or something. We can get anxious or happy or sad, even mad because of TIME. Why?

Is it in a letter, an email, a car, a train, an airplane or maybe a person? Where can I find the TIME to—?

I can't find the TIME. It is illusive! Precious! Unintentional! Disappointing and at TIMES it is horrifying! We have moments when it seems like it has stopped or a blurrrr. TIME marches on…? It isn't a soldier.

TIME relates to all phases of our lives. It's TIME to be born or a TIME to die. This TIME it's love or TIME to split up…? We share a good TIME and then there is a bad TIME. Circumstances again determine the right TIME or the wrong TIME. How about taking TIME off …off of what?

How about a TIME of laughter or a TIME to cry? Time is all about MEMORIES and what will we do next, do we have enough TIME?

When you lose your watch—do you lose TIME? I just took TIME to think about the last TIME

I went to the movies. It's been a long time. I can 't dance, run, ride a bike, swim, jump rope, sing, climb trees, hardly ever drive a car, use a step ladder or go shopping anymore because my body has seen the test of TIME; I've grown old. TIME has caught up to me. How? Where did it go? I'm tired, slow and wrinkled. Once in a while I fall, get hurt, recover and continue to have TIME on this earth. Do you have TIME for more of this foolishness?

Thank you dear LORD for giving me more TIME to share with those I love. Let there be peace and kindness spread among my family and the world. They need to find TIME in their daily lives to know YOU dear LORD, take TIME to teach their children about love for each other and compassion for those who are old.

TIME is up. I've just been enjoying TIME here at my desk. I must get busy doing something or I'll miss the best TIME of the day. I hope you have enjoyed my thoughts about TIME.

December 11, 2018

Chapter 6

Laudable Entries

A Five Letter Word

All these many years she's said she was sorry,
She could have killed herself and she could've harmed me.
Will she ever learn from her mistakes is the question I ask,
But I guess for her it would be too hard of a task..

Too hard to close the bottle with the final twist of a cap,
To end a lifetime of unwanted, uncalled for, unnecessary crap.
She thinks a five-letter word will erase a horrible past,
But that five-letter word can't change life that fast.

I still love her, but truly can't stand to be near her,
At night in my nightmares, I dream I can hear her.
"I'm sorry, I'm sorry," she says over and over,
Knowing in no time she will no longer be sober.

Too many times she has come to close to dying,
I lie alone in the dark silently crying.
When will she get the strength to end all of this pain,
To clear up these clouds and put an end to a lifelong rain.

The time will come when we can see pigs fly.
At night, over the moon, in the starlit sky.
I pray the day comes when she will finally be sober,
Love, joy and pride are the emotions I will show her.

But until that day comes, I'll watch her throw away her life,
A mother of five and was a wonderful wife.
I truly do wonder if God thinks it is selfish of me,
To want her shoulder to lean on and for her to be a sober mommy.
To her there is only one thing I have to say,
"Mom. There is no five-letter word that can make life OK."

By Billy Joe Michel, 13 years old
My Granddaughter

\\\\\\\\\\\\\\\\ **Marry in Haste** ////////////

Happiness and contentment are such invasive things. I have a nice, comfortable home. I have three lovely children and a faithful, hardworking husband who says he loves me. These things are what most people hope for, live for; they constitute happiness and yet, I cannot say I am either happy or contented.

My husband and I have gone through all the ups and downs that married people go through. Our circumstances are better now, we are slowly pulling out of the red. The sad part is, I'm all worn out from the struggle. I have never been the type of woman who wanted wealth. I would be satisfied with enough money to meet the necessities of my family.

There have been many unpaid bills to worry about and quarrels because of them. My husband is a diplomat, he can meet a bill collector and before he is through talking to him anyone would think the man owed us money. That is until the next time, when I have to talk. I despise being in debt to anyone for anything. I cannot lie, therefore I go through Hades every time I am unable to pay a bill when due.

I know there are thousands of women worse off than I am or ever have been. Perhaps I expect too much from life, but I feel so empty and unnecessary at times. I have no enthusiasm for anything. I do just the necessary things around the house and sometimes even let those things pile up. I worry about this because I like order and neatness. I am a young woman, thirty-two years old. I feel that I am merely existing from one day to the next.

All my children are in school now, my time is my own. I feel I would like to get a job, although I have never worked. My husband does not approve of the idea because of the children. I married when I was seventeen, was a mother at eighteen. A mere child in this day and age, no matter how much the eighteen-year-old will deny it. My mother tried to warn me, but like all young people in love, I thought I knew all the answers. I do know them now, I learned by experience.

I wish there were some way to make young people realize all this, but if there is a way, I have never heard of it. Marriage is a very serious exacting job and to enter it unprepared is far worse than taking any other job without preparation and forethought.

In business your boss can fire you for incompetence or laziness. Or you can quit and try something else if you are dissatisfied. But when you marry and have children you have taken on a lifetime job whether you like it or not.

I do not want to give the impression that I don't believe in marriage itself. It can be the most wonderful thing in the world. I am trying to tell young people to think seriously before marriage. It takes more than love to make it a success. It takes untiring effort and courage and understanding, and that necessary evil called money. There is a lot more to that old saying "When Poverty comes in the window, Love flies out the window" ~~ than young people realize.

By Mary Adeline Manwaring Wilson, 1942
My Mother
827 Naylor's Run Road
Llanerch, PA

 I Love Him

I love Him all day long,
And dream of him at night.
And in deepest trouble,
I would always think him right.

And try my best to help him,
In all the ways I could,
Just because I love him.
Yes, I would.

And I believe that he loves me,
For just the way he squeezes, Gee!
And just his kiss,
Fills me with bliss.

And as he holds me to his heart,
I wish that we will never part.
And if I am true to him,
And he is true to me,

I think that when we are of age,
That we will married be.

(MAW—this will be my new initials)
This is about my mother.

By Mary A. Manwaring (Wilson), my Mother
Age 14, 1924 -1926
They married in 1929

sssssssssss **The Women** sssssssssssss

I know a woman who is alive but is not living. She is married and has children, a hard-working husband, and a nice home. She and her husband were childhood sweethearts. As a child, she was highly emotional. In fact, throughout her entire life, she has been a dreamer.

She is capable of doing any job well but must be in the mood. She has no system and realizes it. Her home is either very orderly or very upset, depending on her mood. She despises disorder but hasn't enough gumption to do anything about it nine tenths of the time.

You can conclude that this woman is lazy, maybe you are right, but read on. Her neighbors know her as a woman who can be called on at any moment to lend a helping hand. She would clean her neighbor's house from top to bottom, thoroughly, if they were sick, while her own home might be screaming for attention.

She would share her last crust of bread with anyone in need. People who knew this have taken advantage of her and she knew it, but that didn't stop her. She has an undying faith in everyone, sees only the good in them. One day she is on top of the world, the next, in the depths of despair.

This woman loves music and art and people. She has an overwhelming inferiority complex, that began as a child and has flourished through the years. She is very lonely. Her friends think her a happy - go - lucky, devil - may - care sort of person. In reality she worries incessantly, is forever seeking contentment and peace of mind, and never finding it.

This is the woman whom I know is alive, but who is not living. I should know her, for I am that woman.

Anonymous

****** "On My Own" ******

Just a little note to say,

I'm thinking on my own today.

No worries or voices in my head,

From radio, TV, or things that have been said.

I'm sitting in a room, laughing at the joke.

Those things are just as horridly good as they can be.

Just a little note to say, Today.

I'm glad my mind has not yet gone astray.

By Wendy Michel,
my granddaughter

More to death than just dying,
When you've spent your lifetime giving,
There is no time for crying.

By Mary Adeline Manwaring Wilson

You Tell on Yourself

You tell on yourself by the friends you seek,
By the very manner in which you speak,
By the way you employ your leisure time,
By the use you make of dollar and dime.

You tell on yourself by the things you wear,
By the spirit in which your burdens you bear,
By the type of things at which you laugh,
By the music you buy on your behalf.

You tell what you are by the way you walk,
By the things of which you delight to talk,
By the manner in which you can bear defeat,
By so simple a thing as how you eat.

By the books you choose from the library shelf,
By these and more, you tell on yourself.

Author Unknown

Grudges

Grudges are like pot-holes in a nearby road,
Without repair, they only get worse!
Eating away at the overlooked good part.

Grudges, putting off until tomorrow,
Lets the HOLE grow even bigger,
And the cost is so much more to fix,

We need to call on Jesus, from way up above.
He promises us forgiveness,
He showers us with His LOVE.

Three years have dragged on by,
And holding GRUDGES only makes a deeper wedge,
No one's perfect, no one seems to try.

Do you realize that you've missed an opportunity,
To share in knowing, loving, lauging with,
Those who gave you life?

The agony continues to eat away until,
Our family makes a willful choice to put away,
Those GRUDGES that make us very ill.

Your old and ailing parents long to see changing hearts,
Between siblings, maybe there's a few,
Who want to fix that road, before their parents do depart?

Make this a **MERRY** Christmas!

Written with an abundnce of LOVE,
Mom and Dad, 2023

*************** **Fork** ****************

There was a young woman who had been diagnosed with a terminal illness and had been given three months to live. So, as she was getting her things "in order," she contacted her pastor and had him come to her house to discuss certain aspects of her final wishes.

She told him which songs she wanted sung at the service, what scriptures she would like read and what outfit she wanted to be buried in. Everything was in order and the pastor was preparing to leave when the young woman suddenly remembered something very important to her. "There's one more thing," she said excitedly.

What's that?" the pastor replied. "This is very important," the young woman continued. "I want to be buried with a fork in my right hand." The pastor stood looking at the young woman, not knowing quite what to say, "That surprises you, doesn't it,' the young woman asked.

"Well, to be honest, I'm puzzled by the request," said the pastor. The young woman explained. "My grandmother once told me this story, and from there on out, I have always done so. I have also always tried to pass along its message to those I love and those who need encouragement.

In all my years of attending church socials and potluck dinners, I always remember that when the dishes of the main course were being cleared, someone would inevitably lean over and say, "Keep your fork." It was my favorite part because I knew that something better was going to come ~like velvety chocolate cake or deep-dish apple pie! Something wonderful and with substance!' So, I just want people to see me there, in that casket with a fork in my hand and I want them to wonder, 'What's with the fork?' "Then I want you to tell them, 'Keep your fork ~ the best is yet to come.'

The pastor's eyes welled up with tears of joy, as he hugged the young woman good-bye. He knew this would be one of the last times he would see her before her death. But he also knew that the young woman had a better grasp of what heaven would be like than many people twice her age, with twice as much experience and knowledge. She KNEW that something better was coming.

At the funeral people were walking by the young woman's casket and they saw the pretty dress she was wearing and the fork in her right hand. Over and over, the pastor heard the question "What's with the fork?"

And over and over he smiled. During his message, the pastor told the people of the conversation he had with the young woman, shortly before she died. He also told them about the fork and about what it symbolized to her. The pastor told the people how he could not stop thinking about the fork and told them that they probably would not be able to stop thinking about it either. He was right! So, the next time you reach down for your fork, let it remind you ever so gently that," the best is yet to come."

Friends are a very rare jewel, indeed. They make you smile and encourage you to succeed. They lend an ear; they share a word of praise and they always want to open their hearts to us. Show your friends how much you care. Remember to always be there for them, even when you need them more. For you never know when it may be their time to,

"Keep your fork."

Cherish the time you have, and the memories you share … being friends with someone is not an opportunity, but a sweet responsibility.

Send this to everyone you consider a FRIEND even if it means sending it back to the person who sent it to you. And "KEEP YOUR FORK. THE BEST IS YET TO COME."

Author unknown

Epilogue

Biography of Barbara Lee Laubert

I was born on June 23, 1933, a Friday, named Barbara Lee Wilson, whose parents are Franklin David WIlson, Jr. and Mary Adeline Manwaring Wilson. I have one brother who is 4 years older than me, his name is Edmond Crawford Wilson (Buddy). My sister Mary Eleanor Wilson came when I was two. We all lived at 1512 Robinson Avenue in Manoa, PA.

Summer Sundays Daddy would often take us to Ocean City, New Jersey to enjoy the beach where we watched people flying kites by the water's edge. This drive was about 60 miles away from home. A really big trip, in those days back in the 1930's and 40's.

My daddy started his motor repair business in our basement on Robinson Avenue. Daddy would strip all the wires off the armatures and completely rebuild them.

We lived there until I was seven-years old. The little business grew to be big enough so that Daddy was able to move the whole shop into the third floor of the Wilford Building in downtown Philadelphia, PA, we moved to 827 Naylor's Run Rd. in Llanerch, PA.

I contracted some kind of germ that played havoc with my lungs. Fifth and sixth grade were awful. Mama was forever making a tent in my bed and I'd have to be in there with a vaporizer going to help me breathe. This ailment eventually landed me in a boarding school in Tampa, Florida where it was warm weather, so I could get well. I lived at The Academy of the Holy Names for the next two semesters of grammar school. The nuns took good care of me and I became very interested in the Catholic faith. I remember feeling like I hoped I would marry a Catholic man.

The summer of 1946 our family moved to Egg Harbor City, New Jersey. A new school, new friends, new neighbors, and I felt like I was out of place. I never felt like I fit in. When I was 15 I got a job working at the corner ice cream store, right near my house.

One night when I was leaving work a boy I knew asked to take me home. I went with him, but he didn't take me home. He drove to a secluded area, pulled a knife out and held it at my neck. He raped me! I told my mom ~ she told my dad. My father shipped me off to Philadelphia the next day, to live with my aunt for the next five months. This traumatic experience never leaves you. Fortunately I was able to go back home that summer. I continued 11th and 12th grade in the same high school I had attended before.

I graduated from Egg Harbor high in 1951. My dad put the down payment on a new 1951 blue Rambler American convertible. I had to make the payments, so I worked in my dad's factory winding armatures.

On August 14th, 1951 I met Any Laubert, the 3 star athlete from our high school in 1948. He came over to my car and said, "When are you going to take me for a ride in your car?" I did, and then we had one more date and we fell in love! We were married on February 16th, 1952. Any was in the Navy and had to spend the next year and a half away. I lived with his parents whom I hardly knew.

Over the years since our marriage I had nine children in 11 years, by the time I was 30 years of age. My husband Andy physically built us two homes and remodeled two more homes for us in his spare time.

When the children were getting older, the challenges began to be quite serious. Not with all of them, but I had two ~ a boy and a girl, each had gone astray. Life was changing. Drugs and alcohol ~ police and court were so very nerve-racking. This was so disappointing and depressing. It affected the whole family.

I have had 12 years of tears over my son and 35 years of heartaches and more tears over my daughter. Today, thank GOD they are sober. GOD does answer prayers!

Raising the 9 children presented many challenges with respect to manners, drugs, beliefs and work habits. Including many other problems. I must mention the joys, laughter, surprises and happiness that we all shared with new babies and in-laws.

At one point we had a German exchange student who lived with us for almost a year. That gave us 10 children at home to cook, clean and wash for on a daily basis, plus I went to work on top of it all.

Also, I helped with taking care of my dad plus my father-in-law and then my mother-in-law until they passed in our home. Our children were also involved with helping us, which meant a great deal to Andy and me.

I worked fourteen years as a bank teller, had my own business making bridal party and prom gowns and lastly was a hotel revenue auditor during my last working years. I retired from the Showboat Hotel and Casino in 1993.

We settled here in Lexington, Georgia in 1993. Andy had come to Lexington to help our daughter Lori when she moved here from Florida. Andy felt like he was back home as a kid during his stay. He decided to move here when he retired. Today we call our new residence "Paradise Found."

All of these challenges are *How I Became the Wise Old Lady I am Today*.

After 71 years of marriage, working together on all projects, including raising our children, we have enjoyed a retirement more glorious than one can imagine! We have had the opportunity to travel nationwide and even abroad. I will tell you about how GOD keeps me under HIS constant protection and I have so many wonderful memories of which I hope you will enjoy and find interesting.

February 16, 2012 • 60th Wedding Anniversary!

From left to right, back row: Ruthann, Rosemary, Bill, Lori, Douglas, Beverly and Gregory.

From left to right, front row: Andy, Sr. (Dad) and Barbara (Mom).

Profile

Love is expressed in many ways. It flows from my heart in verse, explaining the feelings that are DEEP. I've been writing poetry since I was a young girl. Inspiration comes while meditating about happy or sad events. I'm an eighty-eight-years-old mother of nine children, 23 grandchildren and 32 great-grand-children. Plus 6 great-great-grand-children.

In my lifetime I've been a bank teller for 14 years, a seamstress (designing both prom and wedding gowns), I was a hotel auditor for 3 ½ years, and I enjoy creating floral arrangements out of tiny seed beads. I'm also called Mrs. Kodak, because I'm always taking pictures for albums, gifts and sharing love.

My talents are gifts from God.

Awards

Of the many poems Barbara Laubert has already published over the years with *The International Society of Poets* are:

1993 *** By Sparrowgrass Poetry Forum
" Quiet Time " // Poetic Voices of America   #249

Spring

1984 *** Award of Merit Certificate / poem …
" Life is a Daydream "

1985 *** A Golden Poet Award
Our world's Most Beloved Poems #582

1995 *** Editor's Choice Award
My Prayer" // Between The Raindrops   #239

1996 *** Editor's Choice Award
I Miss You" // A Muse to Follow #419

1999 *** Editor's Choice Award
I Love You"   #160

2000 ***Editor's Choice Award
"Here's How "   #27

2001 *** Editor's choice Award
Bridges " // The Growing Season   #7

2005 *** Editor's Choice Award
The Bright Road Ahead" // Twilight // Musings #3

2007 *** Editor's Choice Award
"Memories " //Forever Spoken   #1

2008 *** Editor's Choice Award
" Friends // Sound of Poetry

Biography of Barbara L. Laubert

She also wrote a memoir called:
How I Became the Wise Old Lady I am Today (see pg. 181 for cover)

This will Certify that

Barbara Laubert

is a member in good standing

International Society of Poets

**and is recognized for support of
the Society's principles of
Peace - Education - Accomplishment
Charity - Equality**

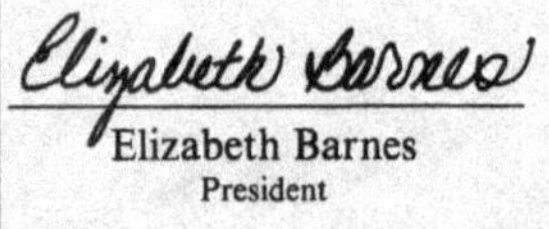

Elizabeth Barnes
President

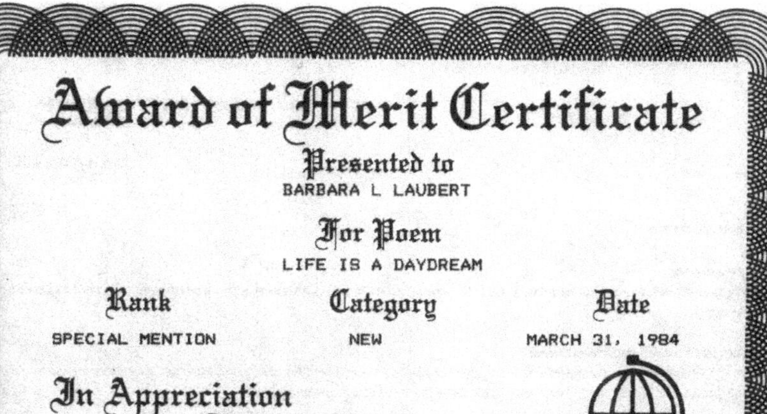

Award of Merit Certificate
Presented to
BARBARA L LAUBERT
For Poem
LIFE IS A DAYDREAM
Rank
SPECIAL MENTION
Category
NEW
Date
MARCH 31, 1984
In Appreciation
JOHN CAMPBELL, Editor & Publisher
WORLD OF POETRY • 2431 Stockton Blvd. • Sacramento, CA 95817 • (916) 731-8463

Golden Poet Award
Presented to
BARBARA L LAUBERT
1985
In Appreciation
Eddie-Lou Cole
Eddie-Lou Cole, Poetry Editor
World Of Poetry
2431 Stockton Blvd. • Sacramento, California 95817

Editor's Choice Award

Presented to

Barbara Laubert

for Outstanding Achievement in Poetry
Presented By
The National Library of Poetry
1995

Cynthia Stevens
Editor

Caroline Sullivan
Editor

Editor's Choice Award

Presented to

Barbara Laubert

for Outstanding Achievement in Poetry
Presented By
The National Library of Poetry
1996

Cynthia Stevens
Editor

Caroline Sullivan
Editor

Editor's Choice Award
Presented to
Barbara Laubert
For Outstanding Achievement in Poetry
Presented by
poetry.com and the International Library of Poetry
2000
Howard Ely
Managing Editor

Editor's Choice Award
Presented to
Barbara Laubert
for Outstanding Achievement in Poetry
Presented by
The International Library of Poetry
1999
Cynthia Stevens
Senior Editor
Caroline Sullivan
Senior Editor

Howard Ely
Managing Editor

This will Certify that

Barbara Laubert

is a member in good standing with the
International Society of Poets
and has attained the Distinction of

Associate Member

for the month of

December 2005

March 18, 2008

VIP P1756131 - 999 1
Barbara Laubert
1026 Elberton Rd
Lexington GA 30648-2109

Dear Barbara,

I am delighted to inform you that your poem "Memories" has been awarded our prestigious Editor's Choice Award because it displays a unique perspective and original creativity -- judged to be the qualities most found in exceptional poetry. Congratulations on your achievement.

Your poem is also featured in a Deluxe Hardbound Edition, which, as expected, will soon be sold out. We have, however, reserved a limited number of copies that are now available only to poets included in this distinctive volume. Because you are one of these poets, and if you haven't already ordered a copy, or wish to obtain additional copies, this is your last opportunity to do so.

Oh, and one final note. Many people have asked if we can make available a commemorative plaque to present their poetry in formal fashion. We are glad to be able to do this. Your poem can be beautifully typeset on archive quality vellum with your choice of borders, then mounted on a walnut-finish plaque under lucite. The 10 1/2 by 13 inch plaques are truly impressive ways to exhibit your work. They also make wonderful gifts. Please see the enclosed material for further information. Again, congratulations on your achievement.